Microsoft

Access

Effectively Manage All Types of Databases

(The Complete Mastery User Guide for Managing Data and Build Resourceful Database for All Users)

Kevin Maillet

Published By **Jordan Levy**

Kevin Maillet

Microsoft Access: Effectively Manage All Types of Databases (The Complete Mastery User Guide for Managing Data and Build Resourceful Database for All Users)

ISBN   978-1-7775976-6-5

No part of this guidebook shall be reproduced in any form without permission in writing from the publisher except in the case of brief quotations embodied in critical articles or reviews.

Legal & Disclaimer

The information contained in this book is not designed to replace or take the place of any form of medicine or professional medical advice. The information in this book has been provided for educational & entertainment purposes only.

The information contained in this book has been compiled from sources deemed reliable, and it is accurate to the best of the Author's knowledge; however, the Author cannot guarantee its accuracy and validity and cannot be held liable for any errors or omissions. Changes are periodically made to this book. You must consult your doctor or get professional medical advice before using any of the suggested remedies, techniques, or information in this book.

Table Of Contents

Chapter 1: Getting Started

Welcome to Microsoft Access. In this chapter, we'll go over the basics of Microsoft Access, making sure you know what it is, what it is used for, how it works, and how you can use it. We'll also go over the various components of the Microsoft Access interface and other information needed to get you started.

A Quick Overview

It's not about generating data anymore; every business is generating data. Instead, you need to take control of the data you have, you need to organize it and display it so powerful insights can emerge. That's why there's Microsoft Access.

Access is designed to work with Office 365 and the new world of cloud-based data so you can see it anywhere. Use templates to build databases faster and create web apps in minutes; everything you need is there, such as Tables, Queries, Forms, Reports, and more to help you add data.

Drop-down menus and autofill recommendations make data entry faster and more accurate, and by creating a web app you can share your data securely and on any device. In a web app, your information is automatically stored in a sequel database so it's more secure, reliable, and scalable than ever. New database templates have an attractive easy-to-use interface and offer a consistent user experience so you can stop worrying about your users getting lost in the numbers. With multiple user access and permission settings, you can manage and monitor your Access web apps through a SharePoint site.

What Is Microsoft Access?

Microsoft Access is a database management software that allows you to store an incredible amount of information and then you can create relationships between that information. So, this makes it easier to find or sort what you're looking for and it makes it simpler to use.

Why Choose Access Over Excel?

Now one of the first questions you might have been: why would I use something like Access? I could just enter information into an Excel spreadsheet; why would I ever need to use a database?

What you might find after you start to learn about Microsoft Access is that some of the things, you're doing in Microsoft Excel might be best suited in Microsoft Access.

In Microsoft Excel, you can track information here as well. Let's say you want to track orders for a company, you have customer information on the left and the order information over on the right-hand side; so, this works too. Well, it's not that efficient at tracking this information.

Let's say that a return customer places another order and you want to enter this information. You'll have to enter another row with his new order, and that means you'll take all of the customer information, paste it down in the new row, and then enter in the additional order details. This is what's referred to as a Flat File; there are no relationships between this data and it's inefficient, as you've had to copy the customer's data from up there and you've had to paste it in again. So right now, you're carrying this data twice, but with a database, you don't have to do this. You can set up different tables for the customer information and a different table for the order information. Also, with an Excel spreadsheet you're limited to just 1 million rows of data so if you have more data than that, well unfortunately Excel won't be able to handle that.

Also, if you go back to all of the order information, and you want to extract interesting insights from this data, like writing a query, you can do a little bit of that with Excel. You could filter the different columns, insert a pivot table, try to manipulate the data to get an interesting view, but sometimes you just need to be able to write a query and then pull together a report and unfortunately, that's not that easy with Excel; so that's where databases win out.

Microsoft Access is a fantastic tool for individuals or for small businesses that need to track things. However, if you're a midsize company or even a large company, you'll probably start to realize some of the limitations of Microsoft Access. So, individuals and smaller businesses can use Access just as a quick and simple database, but if you're a larger company you'll probably look at other options like Microsoft SQL Server and other solutions that are more scalable. However, Microsoft Access is a fantastic tool to learn the fundamentals of database design.

How It Works

To learn the fundamentals of database design, we will begin by going through the Access Workspace. Here, you'll learn how to build a database for yourself or your business.

You start by creating tables, then you'll go ahead and create an order entry form, this way other people can come in and add data to your database, then you'll see how to write a query so you can extract interesting insights from your data and then at the very end, you'll create a report so you can share some of those insights with others.

With all that said, by the end of this book you should have a pretty good working knowledge of how Microsoft Access works.

Getting Familiar with Access Workspace

Before you jump into Access, it's important to familiarize yourself with the interface to know where everything is, and we're going to take a quick tour of the different areas of the screen that you'll be working with, and if you're familiar with Microsoft you'll understand how these tabs and ribbons work.

Near the top of the window is a large toolbar area, and this is called the Ribbon. The Ribbon is a collection of most of the tools you'll need to use in Access, and it's divided into different tabs.

Just above the Ribbon is another toolbar, called the Quick Access Toolbar. Here, you can Save the current object, and you also have the Undo and Redo commands. And you can click the drop-down arrow to add more commands to it if you.

On the left side of the screen, there is an area called the Navigation pane. This contains a list of all of the objects contained in your database. All the objects that are currently open will appear on the Document Tabs bar, and you'll use this to select which object you want to view or edit.

You can resize the Navigation pane by dragging the right border, and you can minimize it by clicking the double-arrow in the upper-right-hand corner. You can also hide the groups that you're not working on by clicking the bar at the top of each group. For example, you can hide Categories, Products Table, and Sales Unit, so you can easily focus on other tables such as Customers and Menu Items.

At the bottom of the screen, you can use the Record Navigation bar to navigate through the different records one at a time. And to the right of that is the Record search box, which you can use to search for a specific record.

Now let's go back to the Ribbon and look at it in a little more detail. The Ribbon is designed to make things easy to find, so each tab is divided into groups. For example, here in the Forms group, we have several different commands for working with forms.

While you're working on a database, you may notice that some extra tabs appear on the Ribbon with a label above them. These will appear automatically depending on what you're working on. When you try to create your first blank database, you have a table that is opened with it. This table hasn't been saved yet but you would notice that at the top it will open up a couple of tabs such as the "Table Fields" and "Table" tabs, to help you work with tables. As you open up different objects, you're going to notice that this change.

Near the upper-left corner, you'll see the File tab. If you click on it, you'll go to the Backstage view. This is where you'll find the Save options and you can Open your databases from here. You can also Print reports or view a Print Preview and do all the different things that are very similar to Microsoft Word or Excel. To get out of the Backstage view, you can just click the arrow and it takes you back to the workspace.

With the Home tab, you can see that there are different tools. If you click on Views, you have the Datasheet and Design Views. If you go to Design View, you can see it's asking you to save your table and you can name your table here also. After that, you will see the view has changed.

You can switch your views and go back and forth between these views and you'll get to see the differences to those later.

Database designs will often set up a special kind of form called a Navigation form. This will appear automatically when you open the database. Instead of using the Navigation pane and the Document tabs bar to navigate through different objects, you'll use tabs within the navigation form. This gives you a much more user-friendly way to work with the database. For example, the employees at a firm only need to work with the Orders, Customers, and Menu Items. They can easily get to these by using the tabs, and some of the tabs will also have sub-tabs on the right. By using the navigation form, you can easily focus on the objects you need without worrying about all of the other objects in the database. It's a great feature, but again, it's something that needs to be set up before you can use it. So those are the basics of how to get around in Access, and in subsequent chapters, we're going to talk about how to open and save databases and objects.

If you take a look through the home tab and check out the ribbons you get to see everything from "Sort and Filter" to "Records", you have "Find" and then "Text Formatting", so if you are familiar with Microsoft products some of these looks similar. It can be overwhelming when you see a new program like this but we are going to break it down for easy understanding.

We also do have the Create tab. If you take a look at the ribbon this is where you can create tables; you can create more than one table and have those connected through relationships. We'll get to that later. You can also see Queries, Forms and different parts of them. This tab is focused on all the different things that you can create. You also have Reports, Marcos and Codes. As we proceed, you're going to see how to create Tables, Reports, Forms, and Queries.

When you start working with databases, you'll use the Navigation pane to open and manage your objects. By default, it sorts all of the objects by type. If you want to sort them a different way, you can click the bar at the top of the Navigation pane and then choose which sort method you want.

The next tab is the External Data tab. With External Data you can import something like Microsoft Excel and if you have a contact list with all their information, you can bring that into Microsoft Access. As we proceed, you'll see how to do that as well.

We also have the Database tools and this is where you can build your relationships, object dependencies and perform order functions such as Analyzing and Moving data.

Chapter 2: Database And Tables

You're going to learn about the database terminology in this chapter. You'll discover what a database is and what components make up an Access database. We'll talk about how to plan your database, which tables you'll need, and which fields should go in each one. You're going to learn how to create a database and create your first table. You'll also know what primary key fields are and how to enter data into your customer table.

Getting Started

To get started with Microsoft Access go ahead and launch the application and that'll drop you on the start page or right here, what's also referred to as the Home View.

Right here at the top, you can create a new database. You can start with a blank database or work with templates.

Over on the right-hand side, you also see a whole bunch of different templates. If there's a template that matches what you're trying to do, this could help you save a little bit of time and you can go in and just tweak it. There's also a massive collection of templates that you can look at by clicking on the "more templates" button.

Below that, you can search for different databases you might have worked on in the past and here you can see all of your recent databases. One nice feature is that when you hover over right here, you'll see a pin icon and when you click on it, it will be added to the Pinned view. This is just a quick way to get back to the files or the databases that you use most often.

If you're just starting, then you go to create a blank database. Click on that option and before you save it, give it a name.

The next thing is for you to select a location quickly for where you want to save it by clicking on the Browse option. When that pops up, you can go then choose whichever place you want to save it. You can also leave it in the default location right there in Documents and all you have to do next is click on Create.

Now you have your first database open and it will automatically try to ask you to make a table. Now, we're going to look at tables.

This is an important part of a database, so you must know what a table looks like and its components to help you in building yours easily.

Tables

Tables are the heart of any database because they are where the actual information is stored. In the Navigation pane, double-click on the table that you'd like to open, and tables will be marked with a blue icon next to the name. If you've used Excel, or another spreadsheet program, then you'll probably find tables to be pretty easy to use, and they are very similar, but there are some different terms that we use when talking about an Access table. Each row is called a Record. In a table, every record contains a customer's name, address, and other information. Each record will have a unique ID number, and this number cannot be changed.

Each column is called a Field. And each field contains a different type of information. For example, in the table below we have fields for the Street Address, City, State, and Zip Code.

Field Data Types

We have different fields and different types of data that are stored in those fields. The most common type of data that you'll store in them is Short Text. So, when you've got anything that's limited to 255 characters such as a surname, a job title, a phone number, now some of you think your phone number that's like a number but we'll come back to the phone number and why we store it as a text; but basically, for anything that's limited to 255 characters or less you're mostly going to use short text.

If you need something a bit longer than short text then there's the Long Text option and those are for entries that are longer than 255 characters. If you have some notes or some detailed explanations or like a review that's going to be quite a few paragraphs then you would want to use the long text, as it allows for more options there.

Then we have the Number data type, and that's any number that is used for a mathematical calculation. Now the reason why you don't use a phone number as a number is that a lot of the time you would want a particular format for the phone number, as the international format, that's better to use as a text. Also, you're never going to do mathematical calculations on a phone number; you're never going to take all the phone numbers and add them or find the average phone number. You just need it as a set of numbers so that's why you should keep that as a text. Also, sometimes your phone number has a zero in front and if you make it a number then it's going to take that 0 away or whatever is in the front, so if 072 will become 72 but if you want to keep that 0 then you need to keep it as short text. So, you use numbers for anything that you want to keep such as recording how many times someone bought or ordered something or some sort of detail like that.

We have the Date/Time and that's used to store a date and time or both or one or the other. You can use this option for a birthday or keep track of the day that you started at a company.

Currency is similar to Number but this is normally for monetary value, so for your salary, payments, or something that has to do with money, you can use currency format.

We have Auto number and this automatically assigns a unique number to each record. So, it starts with one and then the next trick will be a two and three, giving each one a unique number. That's important for later on when we talk about Primary keys and we'll get to that at another point but you can set it to an Auto number and it will automatically do that part for you.

There are other options available. The Yes/No option means it's either true or false or yes or no; so, if you've got a question that requires a yes/no, you use this option.

The OLE Object is useful if you've got a photo or a music file. If you want a profile picture as part of your database you can use the OLE Object for that.

The Hyperlink data type can be used to add a link. It shows you the address web address for a particular web page or if you're storing a document online.

The Attachment data type is for any other file that's not supported by the OLE Object such as a word document, if you've got multiple files, you can also use this too.

The "Calculated" data type helps you to run a calculation based on particular formulas, equations, or other fields. It's used mainly in queries but you can do a calculated field in a table.

These are all the data field types that you can have in your database and as you create a table, you'll work with a couple of them.

Now you know how the table works, let's proceed with how you can create your database.

Creating A Database

With your blank database open, there's not much here yet but don't worry we're going to go step by step on how to build this out.

Over on the left-hand side, you can see that Access already created a table that you can start building on, and by default, it'll ask you to do it via the datasheet view but if you want, you can use the Design view.

It's going to ask you to save it first, so you're going to give it a name, after which it tries to give you the field names and what type must go into that field. This helps you to set up these columns at the top and what type of data is going to be in them.

Let's get started now by adding some fields to this table. Up here, the first field is referred to as "ID" and you can use this table to track all of your customer information. ID on its own isn't that descriptive, so you can update it to be customer ID. To update the name, you can simply double click on the field and then type in your value. Once you're done typing that in, hit the tab key and that will bring you over to the next field.

Next, you need to choose the data type. The data type defines what type of data you're going to insert in. If you want to track customer information, this is going to be things like the customer's name (the first name and the last name), the email address, the phone number, and all of those pieces of information or all of those fields will simply be the Short Text data type, however, later on when you get to the order sheet and you're going to add numbers and so you'll select a different data type. As you're entering data feel free to look through all the data types to see if one of these best matches the data that you want to enter.

As earlier stated, the Short Text data type allows up to 255 characters which is a pretty good length; so, it'll capture all of the different fields that you want to insert into this table. If you want Long Text, that allows it to go much longer but once again short text should be sufficient.

Once you select that data type, now you can type in the name for the field, and when you finish typing that in, hit tab, and you can proceed to select the data type for your next column. You'll go through and add all of the different fields for the customer tracking table.

If you want to add another field that's going to be in the form of notes, let's say you want to include other information like the customer's birthday, this might be a little longer than short text. So, when you click to add a new field, instead of going with a short text, you'll go with a long text and this should now include all of the different fields that you want to include as part of the customer table.

After you've entered all of the different fields, let's see how you can go back and make edits to these.

So, let's say you enter something in but you want to change the text, right here you can click on one of these field headers and you can very quickly update the text. Also, when you click on one of these field headers right up here, that opens up the fields ribbon and right here you can always go back and modify the data type, so just because you choose a data type doesn't mean you're locked in on it.

You can also adjust the width of these different fields and here if you right-click on one of these field headers it opens up a context menu where you can do all sorts of things. For example, you can hide and also unhide fields, you can freeze fields if you've ever done that in Excel before, it's the same concept and right down here you can insert a field, so if you want to insert something between an email address and phone, you can do that. You can also sort, rename and delete fields. So, you can take different actions to make sure that the table has the structure that you want it to have.

Now that we've gone through and you've created all of your different fields, let's take a look at a quick way where you can look at your fields and also modify the different data types. Down here in the bottom right-hand corner, you can enter what's called the Design view and when you click on that, first, you have to name your table. Right now, it's Table1, but you can make it more descriptive.

Once you finish typing in the name click on "OK". This now drops you into the design view, and here again, you can see all the different field names. You can also add field names here; this is a quick way to add additional fields. Also, on the right-hand side, you can quickly verify what the data type is for each one of your fields, and here too you can click on it and you can change the data type very easily. On the right-hand side, if you want to make your field more descriptive, you can also add a description with some additional details.

Let's jump back into the Datasheet view. To do that right down in the bottom right-hand corner again, you can toggle back and forth between these different views. If you click into the Datasheet view. This drops you back into the datasheet view and you're ready to start adding some records.

Now you have all of the fields in place, you can start adding your customers. So right here, you'll go in and fill out their details. As you start typing in information here, you'll see that it automatically assigned an ID, so every time you go through and add a new record it'll automatically get an ID assigned to it. As a quick note on this, ID is also what's referred to as the Primary Key and this is a unique identifier. So, every single customer record that you add to this table will have its unique identifier, so no two customers will have the same ID. You can also use this primary key to connect to other tables later on and don't worry if that sounds complicated, you'll see exactly how you go about doing that.

Once you enter in the first customer's details, hit the enter key and that'll bring you down to the next record and now you can go through and add some additional customers.

After creating a table for your customers' information, you may want to add another table for order or purchase information.

To add another table, go back up to the top ribbon and click on "Create". Right over here, you can create a new table. If you click on the one that says "Table", this drops you into a new table, and just like before you need to build this out.

Right up there, the first field is called ID and you would want this to be more descriptive. So, you'll double click on this just like you did before and this time you'll call it Order or Purchase ID. For the next field, you may want to tie this back to the customers' table. Once again this is one of the big benefits of databases, you can relate information so you could connect one table to another table. So here you'll click on the tab and for this field, if you want it to be a number data type, you'll click on the number and now you can type in a field name, and for this one, you can name it "Customer ID" since you're going to connect based on that primary key from the previous table. As you go, you can add a few more fields. If you want to include the order/purchase date, select the "Date and time" as the data type and rename it as "Order/Purchase Date".

Next, you can add another field for items ordered or sold and this is going to be a number data type, so you'll give it the appropriate name. Now, you need to add another field for the revenue, this is going to be a currency type and you can name this "Revenue". You can also add one more field called order fulfilled, this is so your other staff can go in and indicate whether the order has been fulfilled or if it's unfulfilled and they still have to package it and ship it. Here you'll click on the field and right down there, there's the option for "Yes/No". So, if they say yes, it's already been shipped, if not, it hasn't, and you'll call this field "Order fulfilled".

The last field you may want to add is going to be a little bit different. This is going to contain the revenue per item and you have all of the information stored within here to be able to calculate that. Here you already have the revenue and you also have the number of items ordered or sold. So, click on the drop-down where you can select the data type and this is going to be a calculated field; you'll see in a moment what this does. Right down here, go down to "Calculated Field" and since the revenue per item is going to be a number, select the number data type.

This opens up an expression builder in Access and you can build all types of different expressions. One way to think of it is like entering in a formula. So down here, you can see some of the expression categories; you'll take the revenue and when you double click on that you see it inserts revenue here and since you want to divide by the items ordered or purchased, you'll enter the divide sign and then right down here you'll click on "Items ordered". So that's going to be the Revenue divided by the Items ordered, click on "OK" and this drops you back into the table view and now you can type in a name for the field. For this one, you'll type in Revenue per Item.

You can now fill in some order details. So, for the first customer, if you remember back on the customers' table, Customer ID 1 is for a particular customer, so right back here in your order table you'll type in Customer ID 1. Next, you'll enter in the order date you entered in an order date and then type in items ordered, and enter your revenue. Now that you have that entered in, one thing you'll see is it automatically calculates the revenue per item. The order hasn't been fulfilled yet, so you'll leave that checkbox unchecked.

After you've finished filling out the basic structure of your second table, once again if you want to rename it you can go down and click into the design view, and then you'll be able to rename this. Alternatively, you can also close this table and it'll ask you if you want to save it, if you click on "Yes" you can now give it a name.

After saving your Orders table, over on the left-hand side you'll see that you have two tables now. You could go up here and close the Customers' table and you'll see that all your tables are gone but don't worry you can easily get them back. On the left-hand side, if you click on the tables, that brings those tables back into view.

You can also go back to a table and add some more information. Now one of the great things about creating a database here is that with the Customer ID you don't have to repeat the customer information. You simply have to reference that ID and then for the order you can fetch all the customer information, however, you have to connect this customer ID to the customer table over there.

How do you do that? Well, at the top go up to database tools on the Ribbon. Once you click on that there's an option for Relationships, click on it. Within Relationships, you can define how different tables relate to one another, and over on the right-hand side, you'll see all of your tables. Click on the first table and pull that into the view. Next, click on the second table and pull that over as well. Now you can see your two tables and you can see all of the fields in those two different tables. At the top of each table, you can see a key icon that indicates what the primary key is in that table.

Remember you have the customer ID in your first table and you also have the customer ID in your second table. Now you can simply click on the customer ID in the first table and drag that over to the customer ID in the second table; that opens up a prompt where you can edit the relationship. What this means is that this value or this field in the first table is the same as this field in the second table, so you're saying that these two values or fields are the same.

Next, you'll click on create and you'll see now that there's a connection between these two. So, this is how Access knows how these two tables relate to one another.

Once you're all done with this, go to the top and click on "Close". This opens up a prompt to save the relationships, you'll click on "Yes".

Importing Data

Along with manually entering data into your database, you can also import it from other sources. Right up there on the ribbon, there's the option for External Data. When you click on this, over on the left-hand side you can see all the different places that you can bring data in from. For example, you can bring it in from a File, from a Database from different Online Services; so, there are lots of different ways that you can get data into Microsoft Access.

Chapter 3: More On Tables

In this chapter, you'll learn how to interact with your customer table. We're going to talk about how to add, edit, and delete information from a table. We will also look at some validation rules, working with input masks, you will understand what the Lookup Wizard does and how to create relationships between your tables.

Editing Your Table

Just like in Excel, each box is called a cell. If you want to change the information in a cell, all you have to do is select it, and then type in the new text. After you edit the record, you can save it by clicking Save on the Home tab, but whenever you click out of a cell, it's going to automatically save it for you. So, if you're making a lot of different changes, you don't have to worry about saving each record, however, it is a good idea to save the last one that you're working on, just to make sure that you don't lose any changes when you close the database.

If you are editing more than one record, you can use the arrow keys on your keyboard to move between records; if you prefer, you can use the arrows on the Record Navigation bar. You can also use the Record Navigation bar to create a new record and then type in the person's information. If you want to delete a record, click the margin on the left side of the record, and then on the home tab, click the Delete command.

Now, normally you should avoid deleting records because it can negatively impact the database if other objects refer to the record. For example, if you deleted a customer's record, it could cause the information in the Orders Table to be incomplete. But if you're just deleting a brand-new record, then it's generally okay.

For some edits, you may want to use the Find and Replace options to make a lot of changes at once. For illustration, we're going to open up the Products Table and on the home tab, click the Replace command and let's say in some of our seasonal products, we want to change the word "Fall" to "Autumn". Type in the word that you're looking for and the word that you want it replaced with.

Next, we'll select the Current document, so it will search throughout the entire table and we want to look for matches that appear in Any Part of the field. Click "Find Next" to look for the word. When you get to one that you want to change, click "Replace" and just go through each one and decide whether you want to replace it.

Generally, you don't want to use "Replace All" because that doesn't give you the option of skipping any of them. So, you should only use this option if you're sure that it won't replace anything you don't want. As you practice editing tables, keep in mind that most of your changes are saved automatically. So, to be safe, you may want to create new records to practice with.

Validation Rules: AND, OR, BETWEEN, <, >, <=, >=

We're going to be looking at Validation Rules in tables. Validation means we want to make sure that people type in the correct information into a table to prevent errors, and a way to do that is to have a validation rule which means that the user can't put incorrect data into a field. When talking about Validation Rules, there are two aspects to take note of. One is the rule which is where we specify what values are acceptable for this field so we give it a range, stating what we want in this field, and then there's the validation text and that is what must be displayed if you violate the rule. Now you don't have to put in a validation text, it'll just put up a default error message but if you want to specify a nice little message where you can give the user some help about what they should be entering, you can create your text for your error message.

So, what are the ways that we can make a validation rule? Well, we use operators like if things are equal to a value (=), or if it's greater than a value (>), or less than (<), or greater than equal to (>=), or less than equal to (<=). Also, this symbol <> is used if we don't want a particular value, so we use a combination of this.

We can also use the operators like "AND" if you want two things to be true. If you want one of two things to be true, either one or the other, you could use the "OR". If you want to write something and say 'I don't want this then you could "NOT" for that case, or you can say "BETWEEN" a range of numbers.

There are other operators and formulas you can use but these are the most common ones that we could use. So let's say for example we've got a high school and we only want the senior grades such as grades 10, 11, and 12. So you could say a validation rule could be 10 or 11 or 12, as the possible values; but maybe you want a high school including juniors and seniors from grades 8 to 12, you could say 8 or 9 or 10 or 11 to 12 (that's one option), or you could say >= 8 AND <= 12, or you could say BETWEEN 8 AND 12. So those are all options available to you for your validation rule.

So here we've got our table for illustration, and we've got some values into it, so what we're going to do is to do some validation rules. Taking a scenario, for example, let's say Division and it can only be A, B, or C. So, in the table below, we can go to our validation rule and say it can only be an A or

B or C. You'll notice that if you click away, whenever you refer to text it'll put double quotes around the text automatically for you,

When you go back to the actual contents of the table if you go to the bottom and enter a new record and state that the division must be division "F", if you click away, it will give you an error message stating that you are violating the validation rule and it will keep on giving this message no matter what you type in until you put in one that is suitable like A, B or C before it's accepted.

You saw the message that popped up was just a random message, but if you want to customize that message in the table below that contains the validation text, you could say something like "please enter a division of A, B, or C". So, you can write whatever you want in the text and that's what will be the error message that pops up. So, when you go to the record and you type in a random letter like "S", it gives you the error message that you put into the validation text. So, the text can be whatever you want but you should give it a type of value that will be intuitive to the user, so that will help them know what they must do to correct that particular mistake.

Another rule that we could have for example is that payments can only be made in a value between 0 and 20000, and if that's the case you can say it must be >= 0 AND <= 20000, as the validation that you want. You'll see that with numbers we don't need to put double quotes around the numbers and the same with payments. So, you could do all these types of validation rules and you have text as well.

When it comes to dates you know you're not going to limit the dates but if you want to say you don't want anyone born after a particular date like 1960 for example, then the date must be bigger than 1960 but remember you must specify it as a date, so you need to say >=1960/01/01. You'll notice when you click away it puts hashes around the date, so that's a valid date and that's how dates work when it comes to validation.

So, there we go. We did some text and some numbers and so what that will do is it will now limit us whenever we enter in those fields. So, when you run it, it should say that there were some violation rules. So just to recap: change the rule to what you want it to be and the text is what must be displayed if that rule is violated.

Working With Input Masks

Here, we're going to be looking at Input Masks. This is a group of codes that indicate the format of all the values that you want in a field that are valid. So, for example if there's a specific format for what must go into a particular field and you want to specify that, you can use a special code to say this is what it must look like.

When we talk about these fields, there are different options available to us in the different codes that you need to know. Now there are two scenarios with most of the codes, for example, there's a scenario when they must have that particular value and there's one where it could have that value but it could be blank; so, we have the Compulsory option and the Optional option.

Furthermore, let's take the scenario of a digit. If you've got a number, any number from 0 to 9, it takes one digit then we will put a 0 as the compulsory code and a 9 as an optional one. So, if it's got to be there, you put a 0 and if it could be there but it could be blank, you put in a 9. If you want a two-digit number it must either be 10 up until 99; you'll just put two zeros there and that will be a compulsory two-digit number.

If you want a letter to go in a particular place and any letter from A - Z, then if it's supposed to be there you would use the capital L as the compulsory letter and a question mark (?) if it's optional, which means it could be a letter or it could be blank.

What happens if it could be a letter or a digit in that particular place? This means in that particular slot it could be a number or a digit; so, it could be letter A or could be 3. If it's compulsory then you can use the capital A but if it could be blank as well or left out then you're going to leave a small "a" as the optional letter or digit.

What happens if it's any character or space? It literally could be anything. It could be a question mark, a letter, or a digit. If it's compulsory then you're going to want to use the "&" or what you might refer to as the "and symbol", but if it's possible to be left blank then we can use the capital C.

There are lots of other codes but that's where you can start. There are other options available as well. So, for example, if you want all of the characters to be an uppercase then you just put a greater than (>) symbol in front of the letters and they will make anything that's after it will then all letters will be in capitals, and for lowercase, you can just use smaller than (<) symbol and that will make all the letters into smaller than letters. If you want to display a bunch of text literally like it is and especially if it's part of the code, let's say you wanted to say A, B, C, or M, at the end of a time for example and you didn't want that letter to be confused with the input mask code letter, then you could use quotation marks (" ") around the letter and it will display the letter as is but if you want to display one character you could just use the slash (\) for that, so whatever's after that slash will be displayed as it is. So, if you put slash L, it won't be the code L, it'll just be the actual character L.

So, let's have a look at some input masks. Let's say you've got Car Registration on your table and you want to put an input mask on that; when you click on Car Registration, you'll see there's an input mask area. You can click on the little ellipse there and it'll take you through a wizard where you can add different input masks, so you can have some default ones that are already set for you or you can set your own.

For illustration, if you have LLL 000 LL as the original code, what happens if you come to the actual datasheet view once you've saved it, you'll see when you click on Car Registration over there and type in numbers nothing happens and this is because the first three characters have to be letters. After typing in the first three letters, if you keep on typing letters nothing's going to happen because the next has to be in numbers. So, after adding some numbers, if you keep on typing in some numbers nothing's happening nothing's going to happen because you've got to be at the place where you need to add letters.

When you are done, it wouldn't allow you to put anything else in here, just that format. That's a nice little feature to make sure that people put the values in the correct format. Now back to the table where you have your Input Mask, if you put a greater than symbol in front of it and you go back to your table, you'll see that it's all in the capital. So even though your caps lock is off and you're not pressing shift, if you type in letters it's going to automatically put them in capitals. That's a good example of the input mask for Car Registration.

Let's look at another example and that is if you have Contact numbers in your table and you always want the contact numbers to be ten digits. Some countries have ten numbers in their cell phone numbers and then they added another one because they ran out so the last digit could be optional, in that case, you could have 10 numbers or 11. With this in mind, if you go to Contact Number, type in ten numbers and you leave the last one blank, you'll see it accepts it, and if you type in the eleventh number, it accepts that as another option. So that's how you get the optional digits.

You could have something like a special code, let's say there's a code that you need, and the code contains one letter followed by another letter, followed by one number, followed by another number, or something else. In that case, you've got a compulsory letter, followed by an optional letter, followed by a compulsory number, followed by an optional number, so you could have that particular input mask over there.

For that, if you save it and you go over to Code in the second table, you can type in a letter, followed by a number and that's a valid option. You can also put in two letters and two numbers and two letters and that's also a valid option.

Those are the different types of input masks that you could get and just so you know, while we are on input masks you saw that the code for capital letters is > and that for small letters is <; you can do that on the format as well. If you put a > on the format, you'll notice that it doesn't matter what you type in, it will always be capital letters. If you go to it and change it to a <, it doesn't matter what you type, it'll make it smaller.

So those are options for the format that you use the input mask codes for that as well, for just those two though.

Lookup Wizard

A lookup wizard is used when you want to limit the user to a certain list of options for a particular field. If there is a list of options that you want to select from, you would click from a list box or from a combo box to select, and these display the available options for that particular field. So, let's take a look at the table or what it looks like without a lookup wizard.

For example, in the table below you can see Divisions. When you click on it, it allows you to type in the value.

If you don't want that, and you would prefer to have a little box or a little arrow there where you click and you can select one of these options, you're going to come to the Division and change its data type to a Lookup Wizard.

When you go to the lookup wizard, a box will pop up that will guide you through the steps that you want to take.

Sometimes you have a list of all the available options in another query or table, if that's the case you would just select the first option and you would go select which table or query it is and select which field from that table where you want to be the list of options. If that is not the case, then select the second option that indicates that you will type in the values you want, and click on "Next".

Next, you can specify what your options are. So, you type in the options in the order you want it to be and click on Next.

Sometimes you could allow them to add other options that aren't one of those you mentioned, however, you can limit the options to the list you entered, and then you click on Finish.

What you'll notice is that the data type changed back to short text. If you go over to "Lookup" Under the Field Properties, you'll see a combo box option, a value list options, and the options in your combo box.

So, what does that look like? When you go to the other table, if you click on division, you'll see there's a little arrow there and if you click on it, it gives you all the options available.

If you want to edit those options after you've done the lookup wizard, then you can just go back to Design in the first table, go to the lookup option and you can change it.

You can also change it to be a list box or a text box if you wanted to, so you can also specify those options.

If you initially said from a query or a table, then the details of that query or table will be here under the value list so you can change it there as well.

Looking at another example, if you have Car Registration and you want a list of all the available cars, then you could use the lookup wizard. Here you can choose to type in the values, go to "Next" and then you can specify the registration numbers for the cars that you want; so, you can have a list of all the cars that you've got on your record.

So now when you select a car from the list in the Car Registration field, it'll be one of the ones that you specified.

Also, if you have a list, instead of going to the values you can get it from a table or query. Next, you'll choose which table you want,

Next, you'll choose the field that you want to get values from.

You can sort them if you want to.

So go next, and click Finish.

Now, you can go and view the data. If you click on that field, you'll see all the options that were in that table now listed over here for you.

To recap: if you want to limit users to a list of options for a particular field, you just click on the field and it might say Short Text in it, but you go to the Lookup Wizard and you just follow the instructions. If you've already done it, whenever you click on that field, there should be the lookup option where you can change the fields. If it's from a Query, you can see what the options are, and if it was a value list, you can see the values there, and you can change those values as well.

Relationships Between Tables

Here, we will talk about relationships between tables and how to make sure that the data that you store in your database tables can work nicely together whenever you do Queries.

Before we go into that, you need to understand how you can set up or create your tables in such a way that they can be used in relationships and this is just to give you an introduction to what you should think about when you are creating your tables.

When we talk about Relational Databases, what we mean is that the data in your tables are linked to each other so that the data is common to both tables. This applies if you don't want a table with information on multiple topics and you want each table to store data on a particular topic or aspect. For any aspects that are linked together, you can create some sort of connection to minimize duplication of data or redundancy. So, there are lots of good reasons to have a relational database.

Let's look at the example below. Here, we have a table about trips and then you can see that this includes details of the date of the trip, the car registration and the drivers' details which includes the surname, first name, the contact number, the kilometers for the trip, and then if the person filled up.

That's great, but the problem with this table is that the section about the drivers has a lot of redundant information, and you've got a few people here that appear multiple times. So, there are lots of data that are duplicated, and there are lots of things that can go wrong here. What happens if you fill in the wrong phone number in one record and it is different in the other record? Or if you want to change a phone number? You have to change it in multiple places and if you delete all of those particular trips, there'll no longer be any details about the driver. These are all anomalies that you can have when you've got database tables like this. There's just too much data and you need to find a way to minimize this. You should have another table that is just about the drivers, where you give it a primary key and you can see that each driver now has a unique ID that you can refer to them individually. Now for all that bulky information about the drivers, you don't need all that. What you need now is a connection; you need to find a way that you can attach that first record to the second one. So instead of storing all that data, you store the Driver ID in the Trips table and a driver can be identified in this table by his unique number in the second record where you have all his details. With this in mind, what you want is to take that driver's ID and form some sort of relationship between the driver ID of the drivers and the driver ID of the trips.

They don't necessarily need to have the same field name, they could have different field names, but for convenience, you can use similar field names. Some terminology that we are going to refer to is that the Drivers table is the Parent Table that contains the parent information of the drivers and the driver ID is what we call a Primary Key that uniquely identifies every driver.

In the trips table, this is the Child Table that is dependent on the information in the parent table and although the driver ID is not the primary key, it is a primary key from another table; in other words, we call it a foreign key, which means it's a field from another table that makes the trip table link to the driver's table. The drivers' IDs have nothing to do with the details of the trip except that it links to who the drivers are, which is stored in another table. So that's the relationship that you want to create. So, the goal is to create a link between the driver ID of the drivers and the driver ID of the trips.

When you do this a little box will pop up asking how you want to edit this relationship. There's also a section over here that says "Enforce Referential Integrity". If you click on that, that is going to tell Access to ensure that your data is accurate and that people don't put anything in there, in other words, orphan records. Now, what's an Orphan Record? Well, an orphan is somebody that doesn't have a parent. So, if you think about that for example, you know that the child table is the details of the trips; imagine someone puts in details of a trip and they give the driver an ID that isn't part of the records. So now you've got this random driver that's been allocated to a trip but you don't have any details about them; that's an example of an orphan record.

If you want to change a driver's ID in the driver table it's not going to allow you because it's going to affect the fields in the other table. What you could do though is to do the "Cascade Update" and the "Cascade Delete". What the Cascade Update would do is that if you change driver ID 20 in the driver table to 21, it would automatically go to the trips table and change all the 20s to 21 or whatever you're going to change it to. So, you just change the driver ID and it will automatically change the corresponding IDs in the trip table as well. The Cascade Delete means if you delete driver number 10, it will go to the trips table and delete all the records that contain driver 10 so that your data has integrity.

There's another thing, the Relationship Type: one-to-many. That's the type of relationship in this scenario, so if you think about the driver table, it can only have one person who has driver ID 10 because that's the primary key but it's possible that the driver ID 10 could occur multiple times in the trips because they could do multiple trips; so that's what we mean by one-to-many Relationship.

If a driver can only ever do one trip, in that case, it would be a One-to-one Relationship because one driver 10 would occur in the driver table and one driver 10 would occur in the trips table.

There are different types of relationships and there are diagrams that show the relationships with their terminologies.

You can see the symbols they use whenever they do an ERD diagram that indicates the relation between tables. When you enforce interference or integrity for a one-to-many relationship, when you click "OK" on that, you'll see that one and that infinity sign which means many.

In this case, you can see it's a one-to-many relationship, in other words, there can only be one driver ID in the driver table for a particular driver but that driver could occur many times in the trips table.

So how do you do this in Access? Now you have your tables, the key thing you must do before you proceed is to make sure that they are the same data type and that is the number field. When you are going to create your relationships make sure that all your tables involved are closed.

Now you are going to go to Database Tools and go to Relationships. When you go there, you'll see the tables are already there now but if they aren't there it would be a blank slate, something would pop up where you can add the tables and from here, you can choose the tables you want to add and it'll add the tables.

Now if you want to link that driver ID of the first table with the driver ID of the second table, all you have to do is to drag it over to the other driver ID and confirm that the drivers' IDs are linked together. Next, in the

Relationship type, choose the "one-to-many" option, click "Create" and it makes that line for you.

If you want to get rid of it, you can right-click and you can delete the relationship.

Sometimes if you've made a mistake in a field, if you want to change a primary key or the details of the primary key, it won't allow you because you've got a relationship existing there. So, you need to undo the relationship, go make the changes then redo the relationship, or you can edit the relationship and you can set the "Enforce Referential Integrity", "Cascade Update" or "Cascade Delete" if you want to do that.

So, that's how you create a relationship; you simply take the one field, drag it to the field that you want, and then when that box pops up make sure that all the details are correct, and make sure that you save it, after which you can close and now you can work with your tables again.

Chapter 4: Working With Forms

So far, you've been entering data directly into the table view, but let's say you want to have other people in your organization come in and add data. This might not be the most user-friendly view, instead, you might want to create a form that makes that easier, so in this chapter, we're going to be looking at Microsoft Access Forms.

What Is a Form?

A Form is a way to view and edit the data, particularly in a table, sometimes in a query, in a more aesthetic way.

If you remember when we did tables, we worked with a whole bunch of rows and columns and you saw all the data, now when you are dealing with other people, they're going to use the database. They might not like your current layout; it might not be very user-friendly to them. It's also nice just to view each record individually and be able to see all that information and that's whether you want to change it, view it, or even insert a new record. So, what you would do is to convert that table into a form; it doesn't change the table, it just means you create this other thing called a form that connects to the table. Whatever you do to the form will happen to the table, so if you change something in the form, it'll change it in the original table.

The image below shows what a Form looks like.

As you can see it's a lot nicer to look at, a lot more laid out, you can see one record in full, you can adjust how the data is presented, you can make the columns a bit smaller, and that makes it look more appealing to the person that's going to use it.

Getting Familiar with Forms

Before we get into forms, let's just get some terminology right so you understand. Over here on the left side, there are little blocks on the side and those are called Labels. They will display whatever the names of your fields are, so we've got the first name with no space and you can see that's how it is displayed there.

The boxes next to them are called Text boxes and that's where the data for those fields will be put; so, for each record, when you move through the different records those will change depending on which record you are in.

Now, let's go into Access so you can develop your first form.

Creating Your Form

To create a form, go to the Create option and navigate to Forms, and right there in the middle, there is a section for Forms.

There's a form wizard that will help you through the process, you can also start from blank. Click on the Form Wizard and it's going to take you through a step-by-step process of trying to find out what you want in your form.

After clicking on the Form Wizard, it's going to pop up a little window.

You can base a form off of a query or off of a table, but for this illustration, go to a table, and then you'll see all the fields available to you and here you can say which fields you want to put into your form and the ones that stay here are the ones you don't want on your form. So, if you want all of them, you can just click on the two arrows there and it puts all of them there or you can just add a couple of them in if you want. After selecting the fields, you want, click on Next.

Now, you get to choose the type of layout you want. There are lots of different options available to you and you can click on the default one which is Columns and click on Next.

Now, it's time to give it a name. Remember your naming conventions, you don't want to give it the same name as a table, you can use the prefix "FRM" so you know that this is a form and you can click on the option that says to "open the form so you can view the information". Click on "Finish" and there you go; you've got a nice little layout all done for you.

Your first record doesn't have all the data entered so you can start adding some information and when you are done, click Save.

If you had to go back to the table, there's a link now between the fields here and the fields in the form. At the bottom of the form, you can move through the different records and you can see all the individual records. That's how easy it is to make a form.

If you prefer to use the Form Design instead, click on that instead. This now drops you into a new form, so this will be a lot easier for others to come into and start adding information and they can also use it to review information. Now because you connected the customer table to the orders table, you'll see here all of the customer information shows up and down below it has all of the related order information. So, if you jump through the different records here, you can see your customers and the orders or purchases associated with them.

Right at the top, you can design what your form looks like, so you can choose different themes and colors, you can add different controls to your Form, you can even add a logo if you want to personalize it with your company logo.

Down in the bottom right-hand corner just like we could do in the table view, you can launch the design view and within the design view, you can modify what this form looks like. Right up here there's a Form header, there are also details and you can see a footer. You can take these different elements and move them around; you can design the form how you want it to look.

Over on the left-hand side right down here, you can also launch the Form view.

If you're going to have people in your organization going through and filling out forms, this will likely be the view that they see. Here, they'll see all the customer information but they won't be able to modify the form. To add a new customer record, you simply go down to the bottom and you can click on the "New record" icon to add a new blank record. When you click on that you can then go through and you can fill out the form and right down here someone could go in and add some additional IDs. This makes it easy to get new data into your database without having to see the tables and all of the details of the database.

Once you're all done customizing your form you can close out this form by clicking on the "X" icon at the top and clicking on Yes to save it, then you could give it a name and once you're done typing in the name click on "OK".

Over on the left-hand side, you'll see that it added a new category so you have your tables and now you have a new form. You can double click on the Form and this will open up that Form again.

Customizing Your Form

If you've closed your form and you want to change a few things about how it looks, you can right-click on the form on the left-hand side of your workspace and then go to the design view.

In this view, you can change the labels into whatever you want, make it just a little bit better to view and it's not going to change the data because the data is going to go into those text boxes.

At the top, you have the header which is what is always displayed at the top, and at the bottom, you have the footer. You can right-click on those areas and you get some options like colors, grids, and other options.

There are lots of other things you can add. Over the top there you can see you can add a logo, a title, or the date and the time. If you want this in the footer you can just click on that, cut it and then come down to the bottom and then just paste it.

If you go to Home, you can change the font and the color of all those different things there. Another thing that you can do in forms is you can change the positioning of these values. So, let's say you want the first name and surname to be like on top, you can click and move them to the position you want to place them. if you want to place the text boxes separately, then click on the little gray box close to the text box and when you move them, it does this individually. So, if you don't click on those boxes, it'll move the whole combo but if you click on those little gray boxes, you can move them individually.

Also, if you right-click on a particular form, you have a lot of options to help you customize your form.

You can decide to go for Conditional Formatting. If you're familiar with Excel, this is the same as Excel, so you can put in a new rule.

You can also change the background of the whole form, as you saw earlier with the background full color, but you can also click on different aspects as well. You just have to right-click and change the fill color of these particular components.

If you want to do it to a whole bunch of these components or all the labels, you can just click on one label, press and hold the CTRL key, then you can click on multiple ones at the same time, so that means they're all selected. So, when you change their fill color, it'll change all of them.

So, there are a lot of options to help you customize your forms and if you're not too sure you can always just right-click over here and see what options are available to you. In summary, you can create forms by going into the Create tab, Form wizard, and once you've got a form, you can just go to the Forms' Design view and change the things that you want to make it look a little bit better.

Chapter 5: Queries

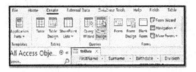

Much of the power of databases comes from being able to run queries and in a moment, you'll see how you can run and also write your query. In this chapter, we will cover the basics of what a query is and how you can make a basic query.

How It Works

In the previous chapters, you learned that tables are the places where we store all the information in a database, we store information about particular topics in different tables and store massive amounts of data. When you've got massive amounts of data, it's very difficult to find the particular data that you want and so that's why we have an aspect of databases called

Queries, and what Queries allow us to do is display just the relevant data that you want to be based on some criteria or conditions; so, you can get just the information that you want and then you can save these results to view them later or edit them or to use them in reports inside.

So, the benefit of queries is that you can take all these massive amounts of data and get just the information that you want. Let's use an example, if you go to the bank, the bank has a database with everyone's records and transactions and all the details of what things that they've done but when you go onto an atm or go into the bank they will bring up just your record, so they will run a query which runs just to get your specific information with your account details and your transactions, and that way they can only deal with yours; they don't just sift through massive amounts of data to find just you're in particular records they can just get your specific data.

When we deal with queries there are some things that we need to be able to use in comparing something to another when we talk about the criteria or the conditions. Remember the operators that we discussed in the previous chapters, so, you can check if something's equal to another by using the equal sign (=). These other symbols will be familiar to you, for example, if you want to check if something's bigger you must use the "greater than" (<) symbol, if you want to find "smaller than" fields, for example, if they paid less than 200, you use the less than (<) symbol, if you want "Larger than and equal to" you use the symbol ">=" or if you want "Less than and equal to", you use the symbol "<=".

Also, if you can compare two things to say that they are equal, you can compare things to see that they are not equal to and if you remember this symbol is usually written as the less than symbol and the greatest than symbol together, making it look like a diamond (<>).

Remember also that different data types need to be referenced in different ways; how do you know what symbol to use for the different data types? Well, let's just review that quickly.

If you've got numbers, you can just leave the numbers as is, you can say it's = 200 or < 200, you don't have to change anything to the number.

That's easy but when you get to text then you must remember to put double quotes around the text. So, if you want a certain field to be "Smith", then you must put "Smith" around double-quotes. When it comes to dates, if you want to find all the dates before a particular year, let's say 2020, you can't say less than 2020 because 2020 isn't a date, that's a number. So, you must refer to dates when you're referring to the criteria. So, for example, if you want before 2020, then it must be <#2020/01/01#. You'll notice there that when we refer to dates you see that we put hashes around the dates; so, make sure that you mention the day of the month when you're referring to dates and then the dates will be in hashtags.

If you've got a Yes/no field, that's very easy. It might seem like it's text but it's not and you can just say that the field is equal to yes or equal to no with no double quotes around, or you could use the words true or false. There are no double quotes or hashtags around it, you just leave it as.

Now that you know this, let's go try a couple of examples.

Creating A Query

Before you create a query, it's very important to know what the data looks like in the main table because if you're going to do queries you need to refer to it correctly based on the data type and the type of information that you're looking for.

If you want to create your first query, it's very easy. You just click on the "Create" tab, go to the Query options and click on Query design. A box will pop up and it'll ask for the table you want to use, so you're going to double click on that and it adds it to the ones that you are using and you can now close the tables option. If you didn't do it correctly and you want to add more tables you can just go click on the "Add Tables" button at the top and it will get you back to the options to add tables.

Sometimes you may not want to display all the fields in a table, if you just want a list of all the names and the surnames then in the table below, you can select which fields you want and then you can run the query by clicking on the "Run" button at the top. You can either run it or you can go and look at the datasheet view; both of them do the same thing technically.

If you want to sort the information, go back to the design view and you can edit this table, click on Sort, and now if you run it, you can see it's been sorted how you want it. When you are sorting, sometimes if you've got multiple sort criteria, it must read from left to right. So just remember when you are sorting, make sure that you get your order correct.

If you want to save this query so you can access it at a later time, you can just click on the Save button and it will ask you to name the query. Like we did with forms, you can add a prefix such as "QRY" to your data name so this way you know the difference between queries and tables, and once you've done that, you've got your query that you can access at a later time.

If you close this and you want to go open up the query you can just double click on it and there you have all the data that you saved.

If you close it and you want to make changes to it you can also right-click on it, go to design view, and that way you can change the properties here or you can just go through those options available to you for your list and any data that changes in the original table will then also be reflected in the query; so, you don't have to keep updating it.

Working It Out

Using the table below, we want to find all the people that made three payments. So, if we go back to our query, Under the Fields section, select the Surname, First name, and the number of payments.

In the criteria section, here is where you put the criteria so you can say = 3; because it says equal, you can just put the 3 and that's fine as well. If we go view this query, you can see we just have a list of those that paid 3 times.

If you don't want to see the Number of payment field but you just want the names and surnames and you want to use it as a criterion, then you can click on the box under the "Show" section, if you go to "Run', you can see the same data with that field hidden. So, note that if you hide a field and there are no criteria in it, when you go back it'll probably take it away when you save it.

Also, if you want all the people that made one, two, or three payments, that means it must be less than and equal to 3 (<=3), so when you run it, you can see it displays all the people that made one to three payments.

Another example is that if we want to see all those in the outstanding column that was above 1000, we use the criteria of >=1000 and we can see all the outstanding amounts that are above a thousand.

If we also want all those that have more than 1000 outstanding but they have only made one payment, this is to be >= 1000 but the number of payments is =1.

AND, OR and NOT

What happens if you have multiple criteria in the same field?

If we've got two criteria and you want them both to be true, then we're going to use an operator called the "AND" operator. So, you'll put "AND" between the two criteria.

If you want either one criterion or the other criteria, then we would use the "OR" criteria.

What happens if there is a criterion that you want but you want the opposite? In that case, you can use the "NOT".

So, let's use a couple of examples using these operators.

Let's say you want to find a value between 1000 and 1500. If that's the case, then you want your outstanding to be >=1000 AND <=1500. If you run that query, you can see all the outstanding amounts between those two values, there's nothing above 1500 and there's nothing below 1000. Those are the types of things that you can do with an "AND".

In the Division field, let's say you want only those in division A or C, this means they can't be in both A and C at the same time; it can either be one or the other. If you say A or C, it puts it in double-quotes for you and when you run this query, you get values that fall under A or C.

For the number of payments, let's say you only want those who made 1, 3, or 7 payments, you can say it's a 1 or 3 or 7. When you run it, only the 1s, 3s or 7s will be displayed.

Now let's say you want all those that did not make 3 payments so you could either say <= 3 or not =3 and if you run that you'll get the same results.

LIKE and NULL

Let's take this scenario where you've got a field that has different types of car models. You can see it's a text field and it's got a lot of information including the year the car was made, as well as the type of car it is and what type of fuel it uses. This is a whole lot of information in one field but the problem is if you want to find just the cars in 2019 (for example), that's going to be difficult because you can't say where the car model equals 2019. In this case, we're going to have to use the "LIKE" operator with wildcards.

First of all, let's learn what a wild card is. The first wildcard is the Star symbol (*). This is the symbol for nothing or anything. So, when you put this symbol in a query, you are saying that it can be replaced by anything or nothing. So, if you are looking for all the cars in 2019, you know that the value starts with 2019. So, this can be written as 2019* and this would be displayed as all the fields that have 2019 at the beginning and something or nothing after it, that is: LIKE "2019*"

Now if you type that into criteria or condition for query, it will put in automatically the "LIKE" for you and the double quotes around it, you can type it in yourself but that's what the "LIKE" does; it doesn't equal 2019*, it's like 2019*. So, the function of the "LIKE" operator is to indicate that you used the wild card.

What happens when you don't want what's in front of a word but you just want the back of the word?

In the above example, if you want to have the word Petrol, you'll just have a star symbol for anything and then the word

Petrol; *Petrol, and then the like will be put in for you with the quotes around it.

Grouping in Queries

Looking at the table below, you can see it's been grouped according to the married field and in the next field, we've got the average of the Outstanding Field for each group. This query gives a summary of the outstanding field, based on each particular grouping. So, the value is telling us that's the average amount outstanding for all the groups that are married and then the bottom value is the amount or the average amount outstanding by the people that are not married. So that's how we can create statistics and we can group data and get statistics on those different groupings.

The table below shows another grouping that we can look at and, in this case, you can see that there is a Division (A, B, and C), and then we've also got "Married" as part of the grouping. In this case, we've grouped it first by division and then by marriage, so we've got two groupings here. Over there we've got the Paid field in an aggregate form, one scenario is to find the minimum of Paid and the other one is to find the maximum, so we have the lowest amount paid and how much is the most paid, but for each group. What this means in this table is that we have all the Division As that are married and all the Division As that are not married, and you can also see the minimum and the maximum amount paid by the as that are married and the as that are not married. The same applies to Divisions B and C.

This has been grouped by multiple groupings here and we found an aggregate field on the same field but different stats on that same field. So how do we do this in a query?

Using the table above, we are going to create a query, select the data table, and get all the fields. Under the fields, we select the data that indicates if they were married or not and we also select the value for outstanding. You can put all the fields that you want in the order that you want.

For this table, we want to group it by "Married" and we want to find the average of outstanding. To do that, we're going to come up here to the tool called Totals.

If we click on that, a "Total" row will be added and it allows us to group by things. Recall that we want to group by "Married" but we don't want to group it by outstanding, instead, we want to find the average for the outstanding.

When we click on it, there are a lot of available options and because we want to find the average of the outstanding based on this grouping, we click on "Avg".

If we run the query, we've only got two options and you can see average outstanding for the different marriage groups.

If we want to find the average outstanding for the different divisions, then all we would do is go back to our design view and change that field to "Division". In this case, if we run the query, we can see the average outstanding for the different divisions.

So that's how we can group data that is similar and find statistics on each of those groupings.

To recap: if you struggle to see the option there you must click on "Totals", and that's where you get this "Total" row. You can then specify what you are grouping by and the fields you want to find statistics on. You change the group bar to the statistic that you want. Remember to save the query when you are done.

Calculations In Queries

First of all, recall the little tip on tables that stated that you shouldn't store any data in your database tables that can be calculated. Now, how do you calculate?

In queries, you can calculate the values, so you can have a special column that has the calculated value or calculated field and there are three steps to calculated fields. If you don't know how to do a calculator field it is recommended that you follow this three-step program to help you do your calculated fields.

For the first step, in the unused column, that is a column that's not used in your query design, right at the top of the column in the field row, enter in an equal sign.

Next, you are going to enter in a formula and if you need to use values from other fields you can use those field names but remember you must use them as they are spelled in the database. Let's say in this scenario you want to work out the average number based on the number of payments, so if you've paid 100 dollars and you made 5 payments, the average payment would be 100 divided by 5; so, you want to take that paid field and divide it by the Number of payments Field. Now, you'll type in the formula. You can type in normal numbers but if you are referring to field names in those calculations, use them as they are spelled.

The next step is you press enter, and once you've done that some text will be added automatically to your calculated field in the front. There'll be a colon and then you'll have the actual calculation that you just entered. You'll notice there that the formula has got square brackets around it now, it is recommended that you do not use spaces in your field names. If you do have a database where there are spaces in the field names, then in your calculation make sure that you put square brackets around the names otherwise it's going to think that they are two different fields so just put square brackets around your fields if there are spaces. If there are no spaces just type them as it is and then Access will do the rest for you.

After entering your formula, you will notice that there is "Expr1" attached before the colon. You can replace this text and give it your value.

Now, you've got a calculated field called Average Payment and the calculation for it is taking the paid field and dividing by the Number of payments Field.

What happens if you make a mistake and you spell something wrong? Well, a box will appear when you go to view the query. When a box pops up and it asks you for a value for a field, whereas it should get it from the field, that means you've spelled something wrong, that's how you know you must go and correct it.

So just to recap our three-step program on how to do a calculated field:

- In the unused column at the top (in the field row) enter an equal sign (=).

• Enter a formula and if you're using fields in your formula make sure that you spell them correctly. If they have spaces, remember to put them in square brackets.

• Press enters. A text will appear with a colon in front of it, just change that little text that just appeared to whatever name you want to put at the top.

If you know the format of the calculated field you can just type in as is but if you're not too sure, or if you forget, just follow this three-step program.

So, let's do some calculations with the database below and for this data, we want to find the average number of payments.

First, we are going to create a query. So, in the field row, we put the first name and surname, the payment field, and the number of payments.

In the next column, we're going to put an equal sign (=), type in our formula, so we take the paid field divided by the number of payment fields (but remember it must be spelled the same), we press enter and it will put in the Expr1 and the fields in square brackets. At this point, you can replace that word with yours, then we run the query and we can see the average payment for each name.

If you want to change that value, go to the column, right-click on it, go to properties and you can change that format to some sort of decimal number or currency.

If you want to add in a VAT column, let's say you want to find the VAT amount on how much they've paid which is 15 percent of the payments, so what you'll have in the next column is =15/100*Paid.

You can press enter or click away, change that to the amount, and if you run it, you can see that there's a display of the VAT amount which you can change to a currency as well. So, these are the steps involved in doing calculations in queries.

Chapter 6: Reports

In this chapter, we're going to look at how you can create a basic report and add a couple of features to it. You'll see how to do some calculations in your reports and how you can do a specific report based on a query.

What is a Report?

A report is a way to organize or summarize the data so that it can be printed.

If you have a table with a lot of data, if you have to print it just like that it would be very difficult to see what all the data is and it's quite complicated seeing it in that table format, especially if you're going to be presenting that printed document to someone else. Instead, you can take that table and the data that's in that table or a query and base a report on it to make it look a little bit better.

The report is very similar to Forms except for you're just doing it in a printed format instead of a form.

Some Terminologies

At the top of a report that's where we put the Labels for the fields so that you know what each column is about, and then the section below that is the Textboxes that will contain the data from the table or the query that you are referring to.

The image below shows what it would look like in the Design view.

You'll see that there's a page header and in the page header you have the labels that'll display as it is, so you can change those and it won't affect anything. However, in the detail section, it has the text boxes which have the actual link to the fields in the table, so whatever is in the table will be displayed there. You can't change these because it's going to show the value for the fields.

You'll notice in your report there are a lot of blocks for each row in the design view. It only shows one and it will just repeat this detail section again and again until it gets to the bottom of the page and then it will recreate the page with a brand-new page header and then continue with those details.

Controls in Reports

There are some controls that you can add to reports which are very similar to what we did in forms.

You can add a label and if you want to specify some other information on the report you can use a label. If you want to connect to an image or show a little picture on it you can use an image component. If you just want to draw a line or separate something with a line you can use the line component. You can use all of these options and we're going to try them now in the actual report.

Creating A Report

Using our database from the previous examples we're going to create a new report. To do that, click on Create and go to the Report options. You can design a report, you can have a blank report and just add values to it or you can use the Report Wizard. For this illustration, we are going with the last option.

After clicking on that option, you can specify the values you want in your report and the fields you want in your report.

When you click on "Next", it'll ask you if you want to do a grouping. We'll talk about grouping as we proceed.

Next, you can specify if you want to sort data by a particular field.

You can also select the layout for your report.

Lastly, you will be asked to give your report a name or title. Remember the naming conventions, and since this is a report, you can use "Rep" as your prefix so that you know the difference between the table data and the report data.

Click on "Finish" and it will show the design and display the form for you.

This opens up in the Print preview option where you can see what each page will look like and you can go straight to printing, but if you're not satisfied with the report, you can edit it to look better. To do this, go to the design view and now you can change things over here.

If you notice that the birth date doesn't fit, you can change the actual layout of the report, so you look at the options at the top and work with those options.

If you see hashes on your report, that means you can't see the data in that field because it's not big enough. To avoid that you can just rearrange some of these fields to make them a little bit spaced out and make them a little bit bigger.

If you want to make it justified or you want to make it left-aligned or right-aligned, you can do all those types of things by selecting Home and seeing all the options over here.

You can change the labels and it won't affect the data but for the text boxes, leave as is because that's going to fetch the data from the table and repeat this detail section.

You can also do other features to your report such as adding another label at the top or editing a particular label. Let's say you want to put a line between each record. In that case, under your Design tab at the top, click on the Line icon and it will put a nice line across. You can right-click on that line, go to Properties and you will see other options specific to that particular line. Please note that anything you do in detail will be repeated for each record that is displayed.

Just like we had in the Forms, you can make your report have a little footer, so you drag that down and customize the footer. You can add your little details and anything that you want to change you can just right-click on it and go to the properties and you've got all those options over there to change.

Calculations In Reports

Before we proceed, you need to know what control you can put those formulas in, and the control you need to use is the Text box. You can add a text box to your report when you design and then write the formula inside the text box. You can't write standard text in a text box; if you want to write standard text then you will use the label as we showed you in the previous chapters.

So, what are the types of calculations that you can use?

If you want to add up all the values in a particular field, then you will use Equals sum (=SUM), and then in brackets, you will write down the name of the field that you want to do the summing on. This is very similar to Excel except that instead of cell references like A1 to A10 you'll just write the name of the field you are referring to. You'll notice that the field name is in square brackets, that's the format is. If you do not have spaces in your field names then you can write them just as is and they will put the square brackets in for you but if you have spaces then just use a square bracket. Another one is the "MAX" which finds the biggest value out of that particular field, there's the "MIN" which is the smallest value and then there's the "AVG" and that's if you want to find the average amount paid.

There's also a "COUNT" where you can count how many records there are, so you can count all the emails for example but because you're counting all the records you don't need to specify a particular field you could just use a *.

The first four functions can only be used with numerical fields or fields that have numbers. You can find the average amount paid or the sum of all the outstanding amounts, so anything that has to do with currency or numerical value, you can use those first. COUNT, on the other hand, can be used in any field, so when you use the COUNT, you can use any field in it or you can use a *.

Please note that you can't use these functions in the page header or page footer, this is because you can't find the sum of all the values on a particular page or some or the max of all the values on a particular page. These will not work in the page header and footer so don't put them there.

If you do want to put a formula in the page header or footer, you can put the current page number. To do this, just say = [PAGE] keyword and that'll give you the current page number. If you want the total number of pages, that'll be = [PAGES].

If you want to use the NOW field, which is =NOW (), that will give you the current date and the time, and then you can format that to display just the time or the date.

So, let's go to the report we designed earlier. Right-click on it, go to the design view so you can change the details of your report. You'll notice that by default it's already added a couple of options like the "Now" and that of the pages.

Let's say you want to find the average of everything in the report, it's ideal that you put that in the report footer. First, click on the text box and it'll give you a label and a text box. To find the sum of all the "Paid", that's going to be written as =SUM(Paid).

Notice that there are no square brackets because you typed just as it is, however, it will put the square brackets in for you. Remember to give it a label as well.

You could also put it in the report header, but that's not a great place to put it but keep in mind that we put all our formulas in the report footer.

Next, go to view and in this case, you can use the Report view, and when you scroll down to the bottom where you have the report footer you can see that the total amount Paid is now included.

If you want to make changes to it, go back to your design view, right-click on it and go to Properties. Here, you can either change it to currency or add decimals to make it look better.

Remember to always put in the correct spelling and you can't put the title in a text box, you can only do that in a label because you want the text to be displayed as it is.

This is a basic calculation that you can perform on your reports. To gain full mastery, you can practice with the other formulas.

Reports Based on Queries

Let's take a look at this example: let's say we've got a report based on all the records in the data table below and then on the right-hand side there you can see the city. The last two letters of the city indicate its state, so Texas would be TX.

What if we want only the fields that are in Texas, in other words, we want all those where the state (last two letters) is a TX? And not only that, we want all those where the division is a C. So, we want all those in Division C of Texas.

This is a very specific report that we want but how can we do that? Well, we could do groupings and that could be quite complicated but then we've got everything in that report and we want to report with just that data. If that's the case, then we're going to have to create a query first and then once we've done the query, we will base the report off of the query.

Let's go look at the query. If you're not yet familiar with queries, you can go back to the previous chapter where we covered that.

Looking at the query above, on the right-hand side, you can see the city is LIKE *TX, in other words, all those fields that end in the letter TX. Again, if you're not sure what that means go back to the section where we talked about the LIKE operator and wildcards in our query chapter. You would also notice that the division is Division C.

After running the query, we get a specific set of results and after saving the query we can go and create the report using the Report Wizard. When you start, make sure that you select the query that you just created, and in that way, you can create a report which has only specific results.

Next, we'll follow the instructions, and after we finish, we'll end up with a report for this query and there you can see it's a very small report, there's not much information and as we've done in previous lessons, we'll go to the design view and just play around with the fields so that they can all fit in.

This is how you create a report that doesn't have all the information on the table but only the specific information that you need at that moment.

Grouping In Reports

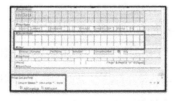

If you have data with different divisions and you want to report on that but you don't want the divisions split up but a more organized report with the Divisions properly arranged, this is where grouping comes in.

So how do we group the data?

If you were creating the report from the beginning using the Report Wizard you would eventually come to this step where you would have been asked what you want to group it by.

You can click on that button to specify which field you want it to be grouped according to and then you have the grouping options at the bottom where you can specify the details of that grouping.

You can also group by multiple fields but one field will be first and another field will be second; so, you can have a secondary or third value for your grouping but it does it in the order that you specify.

What happens if you are in your report and you haven't done this when you created it?

How can you get a grouping when you didn't specify it in the beginning?

Well, at the top bar under Design you'll see there's the "Group & Sort" button and if you click on that a box will appear at the bottom and you'll see there's a little place here where you can add a group.

This can also be done for sorting, so if you want to sort by a particular record and you forgot to do it in the Report Wizard you can specify those ideas here.

If you click on the "Add a group", it'll ask you which field you want to group by and if you select the field at the bottom, you'll see it's added to the grouping. You can still add more groups and add more sorts but obviously, it'll be the next level and then a header will also be added at the top. So, you can have a header for each division.

The key thing to remember for this is that if you are wanting to add a grouping to your report after you've created it, just remember to click on that Group & Sort button. You'll get the option to add groups and change the group details.

Chapter 7: Getting Started With Access

This Chapter will:

•Help you understand why you should keep choosing Microsoft Access.

•Get you started with Microsoft Access.

•Break down the installation procedures.

•Give you a step-by-step guide to creating an Access Database with elementary use of the toolbar.

•Help with your configuration on Microsoft Access.

Introduction to Microsoft Access

Microsoft Access is a tool that allows one to gather essential data. The program empowers users to Sort, Add Up, Recover, and Report results quickly and successfully. Microsoft produced Access and first released it in November 1992. It has the distinction of being the first mass-market database program for windows. It can combine data from different documents by making connections and making information passages more efficient and exact.

Microsoft Access (MS Access) empowers one to deal with critical data from a single database record.

With these documents, one can utilize:

•Data access page to view or refresh the data.

•Report to dissect or print data in a particular format.

•Queries to find and recover detailed data.

•Tables to store data.

•Forms to view add and update information in tables.

Microsoft Access is like Microsoft Excel in some operations like Editing, Storing, and Viewing of data. However, Access has more features than Excel, which we will explain below:

Differentiations between Microsoft Access and Excel

•Microsoft Access handles both Numeric and Alphabetic data, which is used widely for Collecting and Sorting data for easy Access. In contrast, Microsoft Excel mainly handles Numeric data and records financial calculations and spreadsheets.

•Microsoft Access is willing or ready to yield to influence by being more flexible than Microsoft Excel. At the same time, Microsoft Excel is relatively less flexible than Microsoft Access as it might be adaptable to yield under some influence.

•Microsoft Access is relatively less easy to learn compared to Microsoft Excel.

•Microsoft Access can store a large amount of data because it is built to handle Database storing and manipulation. At the same time, Microsoft Excel has a comparatively smaller data storage capacity because it is not made for storing data.

•Microsoft Access functions on multiple relational tables and sheet data models, while Microsoft Excel works on a non-relational or flat worksheet data model.

•Microsoft Access is mainly used for large-scale and long-term projects, while Microsoft Excel is suitable for small-scale projects and short-term solutions.

•Microsoft Access is more accurate and efficient than Microsoft Excel as it limits speed and accuracy.

•Microsoft Access allows the user to decide on the functional data templates and entry forms, while Microsoft Excel works with the available data screen.

•Microsoft Access allows multiple users to work on the same database file and lock data only on the record level. In contrast,

Microsoft Excel locks the whole spreadsheet and allows only one user to work with it simultaneously.

The above references highlight the chief differences between Microsoft Access and Microsoft Excel.

Components of Microsoft Access

Microsoft Access is made of some components which are as follows:

Tables

Tables are vital articles in the Access file. They are comprised of rows and columns and are considered a direct passage into their matrices, known as grids, and contain data that is put away in the Database.

The Row is a record that contains a singular data piece making up a particular record and also alludes to fields comprised of ordered information. The Column is a record field consisting of categorized information. Data can be sorted, imported, or rendered into an access table. Various tables can be in a single file connected through queries, reports, and forms. One Database that includes all the data of one project can be created by users. This Database is known as a flat database.

Creating Tables

The user can create tables in several ways, such as:

☐   Design view

☐   Using Query Wizard

Using a table wizard or entering data, the user decides how to create a table by highlighting it and selecting OPEN in the file's object box. The data entry follows after table creation.

After entering the first record, hit the enter button, and the following line will appear for data entry of the second record, and so on. After the user has entered the data, they can close the table just like any window is closed. The table is saved under OBJECT and TABLE in the file object list. After opening the file, the file object list will always appear.

Relational Database

In Relational Database, the user can easily place a project in different tables assigned to another aspect of the project. The user can connect each table, referred to as a relational database. In summary, when the data in one table is related to other tables, it is referred to as a relational database.

Tables can be related in 3 different ways, which the user can use to cross-reference information between tables. The ways include one-to-one, one-to-many or many-to-many.

☐   One-to-One

In simple terms, a one-to-one relationship is between two entities, A and B, in which one element of A is associated with an element of B. That is, one record in a table is associated or linked to exactly one record in another table and vice versa.

☐ One-to-Many

A 'one-to-many relationship' involves two entities, A and B, in which an element of A is associated with several elements of B. Yet, B is only linked to one element of A. So, for example, one Row in table A may be linked to many rows in table B, but one Row in table B is only connected to one Row in table A.

☐ Many-to-Many

In a many-to-many relationship, more than one record in a table is associated with more than one record in another table. For example, a record in table A is related to many in table B, and table B is associated with more than one record in table A.

Forms

Forms are designed mainly for data input or display. They are used to create a user interface for a database application. Forms are used most often because they easily guide people towards date entering, modifying, and viewing records.

While entering a form field, the field type you set when creating the form should be extensively considered. Any attempt to insert data that does not satisfy the field type will fail.

Kinds of Forms

The two major types of forms are:

1.Bound Forms: Bound forms are connected to some underlying data source, such as a table, Query, or SQL statement, which is to be filled out or used to edit data in a database.

2.Unbound Forms: Unbound forms are not connected to underlying records and could be dialog boxes, switchboards, or navigation forms.

Macros

A macro device permits you to add usefulness to forms, reports, and controls. They are really not quite the same as forms in Excel or MS Word. When database objects like tables, forms, and reports are made, Macros can track down a simple method for tying them together and make a straightforward database application.

Here are some of the main features of the Macro Builder.

•Program Flow: Makes more decipherable macros with remark lines and groups of activities.

•Conditional Statements: Allow for more complex logic execution with support for nested If/Else/Else.

•IntelliSense: While composing articulations, IntelliSense recommends potential values and allows you to choose the right one.

•Easier Sharing: Duplicate a macro, and afterward glue it as XML into an email, newsgroup post, blog, or code test site.

•Keyboard Shortcuts: Involves key blends for quicker, more straightforward macro composition.

•Action Catalogue: Macro activities are coordinated by type and accessible.

•Macro Reuse: The Activity Inventory shows different macros you have made, allowing you to duplicate them into the one you're chipping away at.

Creating a Standalone Macro

Utilizing the accompanying advances, An independent macro item can be made under MACROS in the route sheet/Navigation pane. It is feasible to reuse independent Macro in many spots. By calling Macro from different Macros, you can keep away from the reiteration of codes in various areas.

To create a Standalone macro:

SELECT MACRO under the Macro and code group on the create tab.

Locate the Quick Access toolbar and select save.

Type a name for the Macro, and Select OK on the save as dialog box.

Adding Actions to a Macro

To add action to a Macro:

On the ADD NEW ACTION list select Action

Move the action from the action catalog to the macro pane.

Double-Select the action in the "Action Catalogue".

Assuming no activity or block is chosen in the macro sheet, Microsoft Access adds

New Activities to the furthest limit of the Macro.

Assuming an activity is chosen in the macro sheet, New Activity is incorporated by Microsoft Access just underneath the chosen one.

If a Group, If, Else If, Else, or Sub macro block is chosen in the macro sheet, New Activities are added to the block by Microsoft Access.

To duplicate the activity from an independent macro into an ongoing Macro, you can right-tap on the bartering index and add a duplicate of the Macro as opposed to making a 'heap macro' activity.

Macros are recorded in this database hub of the activity list on the off chance that at least one has been made.

Queries

The solicitation for data results and activity on data is known as Query. The Query performs many undertakings, such as responding to a straightforward inquiry, joining data from various tables, and adding, changing, or erasing data tables.

 A query can assist you with applying a channel to a table's data to get the data you need. The expansion in table data makes it unimaginable for Clients to choose explicit records from the table.

Select Inquiries assist you with recovering data from a table and make computations, while Questions that add, change or erase data are called Activity Inquiries.

Types of Queries and Their Uses

•Append Queries: Used for copying records from one table to another.

•Make-Table Queries: Used for making sub-tables from the main table.

•Delete Query: Used to remove content from a table permanently.

•Update Queries: Used for adding information to a table.

•Select Queries: Used to extract specific information from a large information table.

The intermediate section of this book will explain how to create and use a query.

REPORT

The process of labeling, sorting, summarizing, and grouping data is known as a report. Information retrieved or stored is usually embedded in a report. The tables that provide the underlying data are known as the report's record source, and if the fields you want to include exist in all tables, they become the record source.

We will discuss Reports more extensively in the intermediate section of the book.

Creating a Simple Access Database

Microsoft Access consists of two different types of Databases, which include:

•Flat File Database: This database stores data as text files and can't accommodate multiple tables.

•Relational Database: This database stores data in forms that relate to each other.

.

Before going into how databases are created, it is essential to get familiar with the different data types used in Microsoft Access.

•The attachment stores file like images.

•Auto Number is used when a new record is created.

•Calculated gives an expression that uses data from one or multiple fields.

•Currency stores currency value in four decimal places.

•Yes/No stores only Yes or No values.

•Short Text stores text and numbers that are not involved in the Calculation.

•OLE Object saves audio, videos, and other large files.

•Numbers for storing mathematical Calculations.

•Long text is used for lengthy alphanumeric data.

•Date/Time stores date and time information for a year range.

•All Microsoft database files are stored with the extension .mdb. A database should have separate tables for every primary subject and duplicate data in multiple tables.

There are three primary ways to create a database:

•Database Wizard:

Select New under file after starting the application

The New Record task pane gives you fast access to any database you have dealt with as of late and permits you to make another database.

Select the Databases Tab on the task pane.

Double-Select the Contact Management icon.

Access prompts you to type in a file name for your new Database.

Type Contacts and Select Create.

The first screen of the Database Wizard appears and describes the Database it will create for you.

Select Next to continue

The following screen of the Database Wizard shows up. This dialog box shows the standard tables and fields that the Database Wizard is working for you. Select a table on the left of the dialog box to see its fields on the right. You can eliminate the fields from the Database by vomiting them assuming you need. For this activity, we will leave the standard fields as they are.

Select Next to accept the Database Wizard's standard tables and fields.

Peruse the different styles by Choosing every one of them. Then, select the style you like best and snap Next.

.

Another screen appears with more aesthetic decisions to make. First, select the font you want to use in your reports. Then, you can preview each of the font styles by Selecting them.

Select the font style that you like best and Select next.

You're just about finished. This title will show up on the heading of all your database reports. The following stage expects you to enter a title for your new Database. Then, you can add a realistic or logo to your reports by checking the "Indeed, I might want to incorporate an image" box, Choosing the Image button, and choosing the image or realistic record.

Type db3 and select next.

You've finished giving the Database Wizard all the information it needs to create the Database

.

Select Create to create the new Database.

•Access chugs along and creates the new Database for you. When it's finished, the Main Switchboard dialog box will appear. The switchboard comes in handy, making it easy to access the Database's tables, forms, and reports.

•Explore the new Database's tables, forms, and reports by Selecting the switchboard form's various buttons.

•Move on to the next step when you have seen enough of the new Database.

•Close the new Database by Selecting Exit this Database in the Main Switchboard dialog box.

•At last! You've created your first Database utilizing the Database Wizard. The Database made by the Database Wizard may not be precisely the exact thing you're searching for. However, you can constantly alter its tables, queries, forms, reports, and pages to more likely suit your necessities. Many individuals make databases utilizing the Database Wizard to act as the establishment for a more redone database.

Quick Access Toolbar:

The Quick Access Toolbar allows users to frequently use commands and a chance to design the toolbar with the commands the user uses frequently. The Quick Access Toolbar, by default, consists of the New, Open, Save, Quick Print, Load, Cut, Copy,

Paste, Undo, and the Redo button, as shown in the image below.

•The downward arrow on the Quick Access Toolbar allows users to Customize and add more options through the customized dialogue box.

•Select more commands from the Quick Access Toolbar menu to access the customized dialogue box, and the dialogue box appears. From the dialogue box, you can choose which command you want to add or remove from the Quick Access Toolbar.

•The Quick Access Toolbar, by default, is available in the top left corner of the software Interface. To move the Quick Access Toolbar below the Ribbon, Select the Arrow Button and Select Show below Ribbon.

Dialogue Box

The Customized dialog box is shown below.

As shown above, the dialogue shows a list of Commands available in the app studio.

•Command Option: You can select commands and use the add or remove buttons to add or remove them from the Quick Access Toolbar. Icons, the displays represent commands on the Ribbon.

•Commands with Icon and no Arrow are the command Groups, while Commands with Icon and a Horizontal Arrow contain a submenu.

•Add: The Add button adds a selected command from the Command list to the Quick Access Toolbar.

•Remove: The Remove button removes the selected command from the Quick Access Toolbar. If no command is chosen, the last command on the Quick Access Toolbar is removed.

•Up: The Up button moves a command up in the order in the Quick Access Toolbar.

•Down: The Down button moves a command down in order in the Quick Access Toolbar.

•Reset: The Reset button resets the Quick Access Toolbar back to the default setting.

•Customize: The Customize button opens the customize dialog box.

•OK: The OK buttons apply the changes you have made on the Quick Access Toolbar.

•Cancel: The Cancel button exit the customize Dialog box without applying any changes to the Quick Access Toolbar

•Show Quick Access Toolbar below the Ribbon: This button displays the Quick Access Toolbar below the Ribbon.

Adding Commands to the Quick Access Toolbar

On the Quick Access Toolbar, select Arrow and Select More Commands.

Select a command from the group.

After Selecting a Command name, select Add.

The command name appears in the Quick Access Toolbar list, as shown in the image below.

Access File Tab:

In the File Tab, the behind stage view is the client's most memorable view in the wake of sending off the Microsoft Access Application. To access the Document Tab after effectively sending off the application, select the Record Tab on the Strip. At long last, click on the Lace tab to leave the behind the stage view and return to the work area. The behind the stage view (record tab) permits you to get things done to the Database, while different orders on the Strip tab will empower you to perform activities with the Database.

•The left side of the File Tab is called the Tab Pane. The Tab Pane contains a command for working with the Database and Access to the backstage view.

Commands Available in the Tab Pane include:

•Save As

•Pack and Email

•Open

•Close

•Launch

•Manage

Object Tools and Ribbon

Microsoft Access's Database consists of four Objects: Queries, Tables, Forms, and Reports. These four Objects have been explained in this chapter and will be further described. Together these objects allow you to Store, Enter, Analyze, and Compile data.

Queries

Queries are more intense than a straightforward inquiry you could complete on your Information base.

This is an approach to looking for and incorporating information from at least one table. Subsequent to building a Question in your Data set, stacking it is like requesting definite data about the Data set. For instance, a pursuit might assist you with getting data on a table, however a very much planned Question can give you more data you probably won't have the option to track down by just glancing through the information on a table.

Tables

A table is the core of any database since data are put away in tables, realizing great that a Database is the assortment of data coordinated into many records.

Although the table stores all data, the other three articles {forms, questions, and report} offer ways of working around it by associating with records put away in the Database.

In Microsoft Access, Lines and segments are called Records and Fields. In spite of the fact that Fields go past being Sections, they assist with arranging data by the Data type. In like manner, a Record is something other than a Column; it is a unit of data.

Forms

This feature is utilized for entering, adjusting, and seeing records. For instance, while entering data into a Structure in Microsoft Access, the information goes definitively where the client believes it should go in the table.

Nonetheless, with forms, you can enter information in more than one table all the while in a similar spot. ease entering of information however working with broad tables can be confounding in light of the fact that you could need to work with more than each in turn. The client sets limitations on the singular structure to guarantee information is placed in the right structure.

Reports

You can plan a report configuration to make it discernible by sight. The report offers the capacity to introduce your information On paper. A report is basic since it permits you to address a part of your information in a simple to-understand design. Microsoft Access permits the property of making a report from tables or queries.

Ribbon

The Ribbon contains a progression of order tabs containing the order. In Microsoft Access, the essential order tabs are Record, Home, Create, External Data, and Database tools. Each Tab contains a social event of related orders, and these get-togethers surface a piece of extra UI parts. The Tabs in

Ribbon likewise mirror the right now dynamic article or data.

The Microsoft Access ribbon is found unequivocally on the Windows' top bar. It contains tools organized by Tabs with a gathering of buttons that assists you with dealing with records. The Ribbon has the essential tabs, which comprise of the generally utilized orders; different tabs seem when you can utilize them.

A few buttons on the Ribbon give decisions while others send off an order. One essential advantage of the Ribbon is that it consolidates those tasks or segment centers in a single spot that requires menus, toolbars, task sheet, and other UI parts to show. You additionally have one spot where you search for orders instead of looking through many spots.

Ribbon Tabs and Components

The Ribbon contains a movement of order tabs that contain orders. Access chief order tabs are Document, Home, Create, External Data, and Database Tools. What's more, every Tab contains social events of related orders, which surface a part of the extra new UI parts, for instance, the show, and one more kind of control that presents choices obviously.

The orders available on the Ribbon similarly reflect the by and by unique article. For example, in the event that you have a table opened in Datasheet view and select the structure on the Create tab in the Structures pack, Access creates the design considering the powerful table. That is, the name of the unique table is put in the new construction's Record source property. Moreover, some ribbon tabs simply appear in unambiguous settings.

• Home Tab: Create a different view, Copy and Paste from Clipboard, Apply rich text formatting to a memo, Sort and Filter records, and Find records.

•Create Tab: Create a new blank page, Create a new table with the template, Create a list of SharePoint sites, Create a new blank Table, Create a new form, Create a new pivot table or chart, Create a new report, and Create a new Query, Macro or Module.

•External Data: Import links to external data, export, Collect updates and data via email, and Load the link Table Manager.

•Database Tool: Move some or all parts of a database to a new or existing SharePoint site, Launch the Visual Basic editor or load a macro, Create and View table relationships, Show or hide object dependency, Load the database Documenter, Move data to Microsoft SQL server, manage access add-ins, Create or edit a Visual Basic Application.

Microsoft Access Security

MS Access 2021 gives the following ways to secure an application while still allowing users to remain active:

- MDE Version

- Database Password

- Workgroup Security

- Encryption

1.Access MDE Version

A database can be secured or locked, and the client can incorporate source code by switching the DB over completely to a MDE document in the event that a database should be locked to forestall unapproved changes.

2.Database password is the essential degree of safety, and whenever it is placed, a client has unlimited oversight of the database objects. This is the most fragile yet the most broadly utilized technique.

Encryption

One more type of security is encryption. The Entrance 2021 ACCDB design gives progressed encryption of more established adaptations.

3.Workgroup Security

This level requires a username and secret key. A workgroup security record likewise contains settings for dealing with numerous databases.

This ends the first Chapter of the book. Continuous use of the listed steps only makes you better.

Chapter 8: Working With Tables

In This Chapter:

•Adding Fields & Explaining Data Types in Access Tables

•Understanding Tables

•All About Gridlines

•Data Types in Relationships and Joins

•Sort and Filter Records

•All About Access Field Properties

This topic is intended for users who have not studied Query Tables or Formulas, whether or not they have a basic knowledge of Access. It includes information on how to start a new Access project and create a new table or query, as well as how to create queries from existing tables and how to modify an Access table in Design View. Concepts here include the tables, fields, and their properties.

When building a database, you store your information in tables, which are collections of rows and columns organized according to a subject. The information items you want to track are kept in fields (also called columns). For instance, you may add Last Name, First Name, Phone Number, and Address fields to a Contacts database. Likewise, you might add Product Name, Product ID, and Price fields to a Products table.

You should be careful when selecting fields. For instance, adding a field to store a calculated value may be a terrible idea. Most of the time, you can ask for Access to calculate the value when required. When deciding on fields, strive to store data in its most minor, most valuable parts. For instance, consider keeping the first and last names separately rather than the complete name in a single field. In general, place a piece of information in a field whenever you need to report, sort, search, or calculate it.

A field has distinctive qualities that set it apart. For instance, each field in a database has a name that distinctly distinguishes it. Additionally, a field has a data type that is selected to fit the data that will be stored in it. The storage space to allot for each value depends on the data type, which also determines the values the user can store and the operations the user can carry out. Each field also contains a collection of attributes that describe the field's visual or behavioral qualities. For instance, the Format property specifies how a field should be presented or how it should look.

Adding Fields and Explaining Data Types in Access Tables

When constructing an Access database, you store your data in table subject-based lists with rows and columns. For instance, you could make a Contacts table to keep a list of names, addresses, and phone numbers or a Products table to keep track of product details. This section will take you through how to construct a table, add fields to a table, set the table's primary key, and set field and table properties. Also, you will be reading about the different data types used in MS Access.

Make sure you comprehend the underlying ideas before you add fields and construct tables.

Creating a Table

Like a contact list, a primary database might just have one table. But many databases employ several tables. A new file that serves as a container for all objects in your database, including tables, is created when you create a new database.

The user can create a table by making a new database, inserting an existing database with a table, or importing or connecting to a table from another data source, such as a text file, a Microsoft Excel workbook, a Microsoft Word document, or another database. When you establish a brand-new, blank database, a brand-new, empty table is automatically added for you. After that, you may begin defining your fields by entering data in the table.

Making a New Table in a New Database

Select the Create tab.

Select Table.

A new table appears in Datasheet View. You can enter data immediately, but you should add some fields first.

Select the Select to add field heading.

A list of data types appears. See the table at the end of this lesson to learn more about your options.

Select the field type.

Type a name for the field.

Repeat Steps 3-5 to add the remaining fields to your table.

When you're finished adding fields, Select the Close button and Select Yes to save your changes.

Enter a name for your new table and Select OK

A new table named Table 1 is created and displayed in the Datasheet view as soon as the new database is opened.

To open a current table:

•Open your database and find the Navigation pane.

•In the Navigation pane, find the table you need to open.

•Double tap the ideal table.

The table will open and show up as a tab in the Report Tabs bar.

Understanding Tables

All tables are made of even lines and vertical segments, with little square shapes called cells in the spots where lines and sections converge. In Access, lines and sections are alluded to as records and fields.

A field is an approach to sorting out information by type. Consider the field name as an inquiry and each cell inside that field as a reaction to that inquiry. In our model, the Last Name field is chosen, containing each last name in the table.

Fields and field names

A record is one unit of information. Each cell on a given column is essential for that line's record. In our model, Quinton Boyd's record is chosen, which contains all of the information connected with him in the table.

•Records and record ID numbers

Each record has a unique ID number that alludes to whatever information it contains. The ID number for a record can't be changed.

Every data cell in your table is essential for both a field and a record. So, for example, if you had a table of names and contact information, every individual would be addressed by a record, and each snippet of information about every individual — name, telephone number, address, etc. — would be held inside a specific field on that record's line.

Select the buttons in the intelligent options beneath to figure out how to explore a table.

Creating a New Table in an Existing Database

After successfully launching into an existing database,

On the Create tab, select the table under the Tables category.

The database has a new table, which opens in the Datasheet view.

Navigating within tables

The bar at the bottom of the table contains several commands to help you search or scroll through records:

•To explore through records in a table, you can utilize the all-over bolt keys, look all over, or utilize the bolts in the Record Navigation bar situated at the lower part of your table.

•You can create another record with the new (transparent) record order on the Record Navigation bar.

•You can track any record in the now open table by looking for it using the record search box. Place your cursor in the pursuit box, type any word that shows up in the record you need to find, and press the Enter key.

To explore between fields, you can utilize the left and right bolt keys or parchment left and right.

Adding records and entering data

Entering data into tables in Access is like entering data in Succeed. To work with records, you'll need to enter data into cells.

To add a new record:

There are three ways to add a new record to a table:

•In the Records group on the Home tab, Select the new command.

•Select the new record button on the Record Navigation bar at the bottom of the window.

•Begin typing in the row below your last added record.

•Sometimes, when you enter information into a record, a window will spring up to inform you that the information you've entered is invalid. This implies the field you're working with has an approval rule, which is a standard about the kind of data that can show up in that field. Select OK, and then adhere to the guidelines in the pop-up window to return your data.

To save a record:

Access saves records automatically. After entering a record, you can choose an alternate record or close the item, and Access will save the record. Be that as it may, in specific circumstances, you may need to save a record physically. For instance, assuming that you want to alter a current record, you could save the record by guaranteeing your progressions are saved.

Select the Home tab and locate the Records group.

Select the Save command. The record will be saved.

Editing records

You can select a record and type your changes to quickly edit it within a table. In addition, Access lets you find and replace a word within multiple records and delete records entirely.

To replace a word within a record:

You can edit multiple occurrences of the same word by using Find and Replace, which searches for a term and replaces it with another term.

Select the Home tab and locate the Find group.

Select the Replace command. The Find and Replace dialog box will appear.

In the Find What: field, type the word you want to find, and then in the Replace With field, type the word you want to replace the original word with. In our example, we'll find instances of the word fall and replace it with Autumn.

Select the Look In drop-down arrow to select your search area. Select the Current field to limit your search to the currently selected field. Select Current document to search within the entire table.

Select the Match: drop-down arrow to select how closely you'd like results to match your search. Select Any Part of Field to search for your search term in any part of a cell. Select Whole Field to search only for cells that match your search term. Select Start of Field to search only for cells that start with your search term.

Select Find Next. If the text is found, it will be highlighted.

Review the text to make sure you want to replace it. Then, click Replace to substitute the original word with the new one.

Access will move to the next instance of the text in the object. When you are finished replacing text, select cancel to close the dialog box.

The Replace All option is powerful but may change some things you don't want to change. In the example below, the word fall does not refer to the seasons, so replacing it with Autumn would be incorrect. The standard Replace option allows you to check each instance before replacing the text. You can select Find Next to skip to the next instance without replacing the text.

To delete a record:

Select the entire record by choosing the gray border on the left side of the record.

Select the Home tab and locate the Records group.

Select the Delete command.

A dialog box will appear. Click on yes.

The record will be permanently deleted.

The ID numbers assigned to records stay the same even after you delete a record. So, for example, if you delete the 205th record in a table, the sequence of record ID numbers will read ... 204, 206, 207 ... rather than ... 204, 205, 206, 207...

Modifying table appearance

Access offers different ways of adjusting the presence of tables, including resizing fields and rows and briefly concealing data you don't have to see. These progressions aren't just about doing right by your table; they can make the table simpler to peruse.

Resizing fields and rows

If your fields and lines are excessively small or enormous for the information contained within them, you can constantly resize them, so the text is all shown.

To resize a field:

 Place your cursor over the right gridline in the field title. Your mouse will become a double arrow.

 Select and drag the gridline to the right or left to increase or decrease the field width, and then release the mouse. The field width will be changed.

To resize a row:

Place your cursor over the bottom gridline in the gray area to the left of the row. Your mouse will become a double arrow.

Select and drag the gridline downward to increase the row height or upward to decrease the row height, and then release the mouse. The row height will be changed.

Hiding fields

If you have a field you don't anticipate altering or don't believe others should alter, you can conceal it. A secret field is undetectable yet is still essential for your information base. The information inside a secret field can, in any case, be gotten from forms, queries, reports, and any related tables.

To hide a field:

Right-click the field title and then select hide Fields.

The field will be hidden.

If you want the field to be visible again, you can unhide it. Simply right-Select any field title, and then select Unhide Fields. A dialog box will appear. Select the checkboxes of any fields you want to be visible again, and then Select Close.

Table formatting options

Alternate row color

By default, the background of every other row in an Access table is a few shades darker than the table's background. This darker alternate row color makes your table easier to read by offering a visual distinction between each record and the records directly above and below it.

To change the alternate row color:

Select the Home tab, locate the Text Formatting group, and Select the Alternate Row Color drop-down arrow.

Select a color from the drop-down menu or No Color to remove the alternate row color.

The alternate row color will be updated.

Modifying gridlines

Another way through which Access makes your tables easier to read is by adding gridlines that mark the borders of each cell. Gridlines are the thin lines that appear between each cell, row, and column of your table. By default, gridlines are dark gray and appear on every side of a cell, but you can change their color and hide undesired gridlines.

To customize which gridlines appear:

Select the Home tab, locate the Text Formatting group, and Select the Gridlines drop-down arrow.

Select the gridlines you want to appear. You can choose horizontal gridlines between the rows, vertical gridlines between the columns, gridlines, or none.

The grid lines on your table will be updated.

Additional formatting options

To view additional formatting options, select the Datasheet Formatting arrow in the bottom-right corner of the Text Formatting group.

The Datasheet Formatting dialog box offers several advanced formatting options, including modifying background color, gridline color, and border and line style. It even includes viewing a sample table with your formatting choices, so you can play around with the various formatting options until you get your table looking the way you want it.

Adding Fields

•Each item of information you want to track is stored in a field. For instance, you might add last name, First Name, Phone Number, and address fields to a contacts database. Likewise, you can add fields for Product Name, Product ID, and Price to a products table.

•You can add fields to an Access table to store additional information about something for which you already have a table. For example, consider a scenario in which you have a table that contains the customer's last name, first name, email address, contact information, and postal address. You add a field to save the information if you want to start keeping track of each customer's preferred method of communication.

•Try to break down the data into its most minor usable components before creating fields. Later on, merging data is much simpler than separating it. For instance, consider making the Last Name and First

Name fields distinct from the Full Name field. Once that is done, you can quickly search or sort by First Name, Last Name, or both. Put a piece of data in a field if you report, sort, search, or compute.

•Every field has a few essential components, including a name that identifies it specifically within a table, a data type that describes the data's nature, the operations that may be applied to it, and how much storage space should be allocated for each value.

•You can modify a field's properties after creating it to modify how it appears and behaves. For instance, the Format property specifies how the data will display in a datasheet or form with that field.

Add a Field by Entering Data

You can add a field to a table when you create a new one or launch an existing table in the Datasheet view by entering information in the Add New Field column of the datasheet (1). Access will automatically choose a data type for the field based on the value you enter. Access defaults to text as the data type if your input infers no other data type, but you can change it.

Input data into the Add New Field column as follows:

You can create or open a table in this view by selecting Datasheet view from the shortcut menu when you Right-Select the desired table in the Navigation Pane.

Type the field name you wish to create in the Add New Field column.

Give the field a descriptive name, so its nature is evident.

Enter data in the new field.

Using a Field Template to add a Field

Sometimes, selecting a field that fits your needs from a predefined list is more straightforward than constructing one manually. You can select a field template from a list using the More Fields list. A pre-set list of qualities and traits that characterize a field is known as a field template. A field's name, data type, format setting, and other field properties are all listed in the field template definition.

Select View first, followed by Datasheet View, under the Views group on the Home tab.

Select More Fields under the Add & Delete group on the Fields tab.

To add the new column, choose a field from the list of More Fields. The field is positioned by Access to the right of the column where your cursor is present. For example, in your table, Access produces many fields to hold the various components of an address if you select one of the field options under the Quick Start header, such as address.

Introduction to Data Types

Data types can be puzzling. For instance, if a field's data type is text, it can contain information composed of text and numeric characters. However, a field of the data type Number can only hold numerical information. Thus, you must be aware of the properties associated with each data type.

The data type of a field affects several significant field characteristics, including the following:

•What formats are compatible with the field.

•The most significant field value possible.

•Whether or not the field can be indexed.

•Depending on how the new field is created, a field's data type may be predefined, or you may choose a data type.

•The expressions that can be made using the field.

•Use a field whose data type has been declared in a template or another table.

•Fill in a blank column (or field) with data; Access will determine the data type for the field based on the values you provide, or you may specify the data type and format for the field.

•When you select Add Fields in the Fields & Columns group on the Modify Fields page, Access presents a list of available data types for you to choose from.

When to use which Data Type

Consider a field's data type as a set of characteristics that apply to all values stored in the field. For instance, only letters, integers, and a small number of punctuation characters are allowed in values saved in Text fields, and a Text field can only hold a maximum of 255 characters.

There are situations when data in a field may look like one data type but be another.

A field, for instance, can appear to have numeric values but instead include text values, such as room numbers. You can frequently use an expression to compare or convert values of various data kinds.

Basic Data Types

Data Type: displays

•Check Box: A check box.

•Yes/No: Yes or No options

•True/False: True or False options

•OLE Object : On or Off options. OLE objects, such as Word documents.

Format: displays

•Text: Short, alphanumeric values include the last name or street address. Beginning in Access 2013, Text data types were renamed to Short Text.

•Number, Large Number: Numeric values, such as distances. Note that there is a separate data type for currency.

•Currency: Monetary values.

•Yes/No: Yes and No values and fields that contain only one of two values.

•Date/Time, Date/Time Extended: Date and time values for the years 100 through 9999.

•Date/Time Extended: Date and time values for the years 1 through 9999.

•Rich Text: Text or combinations of text and numbers can be formatted using color and font controls.

•Calculated field: The calculation must refer to other fields in the same table. You would use the Expression Builder to create the calculation. Note, calculated fields were first introduced in Access 2010.

•Attachment: Attached are images, spreadsheet files, documents, charts, and other types of supported files to the records in your database, Similar to attaching files to email messages.

•Hyperlink: Text or combinations of text and numbers stored as text and used as a hyperlink address.

•Memo: Long blocks of text. A typical use of a Memo field would be a detailed product description. Note, starting from Access 2013, Memo data types have been renamed Long Text.

•Lookup: Displays either a list of values that is retrieved from a table or query, or a set of values you specified when creating the field.

The wizard starts, and you can create a Lookup field. The data type of a lookup field is either Text or Number, depending on what you choose in the wizard.

Lookup fields have additional field properties located on the Lookup tab in the Field Properties pane.

Formats accessible for each data type and an explanation of how each format affects the data are displayed in the following tables.

Format: Displays

•Short Date: Display the date in a short format. It depends on your regional date and time settings. For example, 3/14/2021 for the USA.

•Medium Date: Display the date in medium format—for example, 3-Apr-09 for the USA.

•Long Date: Display the date in an extended format. It depends on your regional date and time settings. For example, Wednesday, March 14, 2021, for the USA.

•Time am/pm: Display the time only using a 12-hour format that will respond to changes in the regional date and time settings.

•Medium Time: Display the time followed by AM/PM.

•Time 24hour: Display the time only using a 24-hour format that will respond to changes in the regional date and time settings.
.

Data Type Reference

A data type contains a list of selectable properties when you apply it to a field.

•Format: Use to display

•General: Numbers without additional formatting precisely as it is stored.

•Currency: General monetary values.

•Euro: General monetary values are stored in the EU format.

•Fixed: Numeric data.

•Standard: Numeric data with decimal.

•Percentage: Percentages.

•Scientific: Calculations.

Data Types in Relationships and Joins

When two tables have similar fields, they are said to have a stable relationship. One-to-one, one-to-many, and many-to-many relationships are the three types of relationships.

When you build a table relationship or add a join to a query, the fields you connect must be of the same or equivalent data type. Even if the values in two fields match, you cannot create a join between a Number field and a Text field, for example.

•Attachment

•AutoNumber

•Calculated

•Currency

•Date/Time and Date/Time Extended

•Hyperlink

•Memo

•Number

- Large Number

- OLE Object

- Text

- Yes/No

A join is a SQL operation that merges data from two sources into a single query record based on values in a shared field. For example, a join might be inner, left outer, or right outer – depending on the direction.

Sort and Filter Records

Access allows you to interact with vast amounts of data. In addition, you can choose how you arrange and view your data using the sorting and filtering tools, which makes it easier to deal with.

Tools that let you arrange your data include sorting and filtering. Data is put in order when it is sorted. And you can hide irrelevant info and concentrate only on the things you are interested in by filtering the data.

Sorting Records

Records are arranged when sorted, with related data being grouped. So, compared to unsorted data, sorted data is frequently easier to read and comprehend. Access, by default, arranges records according to their ID numbers. There are, however, a variety of additional techniques to sort records. The data in a bakery's database, for instance, could be sorted in a variety of ways:

The last name of the clients who placed the orders or the order date could be used to sort the orders.

Customers might be grouped by their names, cities, or zip codes.

The products can be arranged by name, category (such as pies, cakes, and cupcakes), or price.

Using ascending or descending order, you can sort both text and numbers. In ascending order, numbers are sorted from smallest to largest, and text from A to Z. The descending order works in the opposite direction for numbers and text. Because your tables' tables of ID numbers, by default, sort them in ascending order, the lowest ID numbers are displayed first.